D1758395

Walk!

La Palma

with

Charles Davis & Jan Kostura

DISCOVERY WALKING GUIDES LTD

Walk! La Palma (3rd edition)

First Edition published March 2005
Second edition published November 2010
Third edition published November 2015

Published by Discovery Walking Guides Ltd
10 Tennyson Close, Northampton NN5 7HJ, England

Maps
Maps sections are taken from **La Palma Tour & Trail Map** published by **Discovery Walking Guides Ltd**.

Photographs
The photographs in this book were contributed by the authors, their co-walkers and by Ros Brawn.

Front Cover Photographs

Walk 35 Santa Cruz to Mirador de la Concepción

28 Roque Palmero

22 Barlovento to Gallegos

Walk 32 Pico Bejenado

Text © Jan Kostura & Charles Davis

ISBN 9781782750215

Walk! La Palma

CONTENTS

THE WALKS

SOUTH: SANTA CRUZ DE LA PALMA TO TAZACORTE

NORTH-EAST: EL TABLADO TO SANTA CRUZ DE LA PALMA

CALDERA DE TABURIENTE

After twenty years travelling the world pretending to be a teacher, Charles Davis concluded that wandering about mountain tops was a more productive way of spending his time than standing in front of a classroom, a decision that has lead to over a dozen books for Discovery Walking Guides.

He is also the author of several novels, published by The Permanent Press. He is accompanied in his peregrinations by Jeannette (a refugee from the French education system) and assorted dogs that other people saw fit to dump in the local Rescue Centre, often for very good reasons. For more information, see:-

http://charlesdavis2.wix.com/charlesdavis

After university, Jan Kostura set off on his travels, living and working in various far-flung places inspired by his passion for stimulating multicultural environments. However, being a stressed out desk-jockey in a hectic consulting business turned out not to be his thing, so after two years slouching in a chair he swapped the office for a more liberating environment the great outdoors.

He found his second home in the Canary Islands, where he fell in love with the ambiance, the warm-hearted people, the constant sun, the stunning mountains and flamboyant nature.

Nowadays Jan works as a mountain guide, organizing hiking expeditions and adventure holidays, and writes articles on travelling.

PREFACE

Back in 1996, the first of our Discovery Walking Guides for the east and west of the island of La Palma were published. Modest folded sheets, they formed the foundation for future titles. In March 2005 came our first full Walk! La Palma book and the first edition of La Palma Tour & Trail Super-Durable Map.

The research back then was all completed by David and Ros Brawn though as DWG grew it was clear that we needed to find walking author/researchers. In the case of La Palma, Charles Davis proved to be the ideal choice, walking the island in 2005 and providing updates and new information for another edition in 2010. In the meantime, La Palma Tour & Trail Maps for the island have continued to evolve, the most recent being edition five.

Now we're pleased to welcome a new author/researcher on board for this 3rd edition of Walk! La Palma. Jan Kostura and Charles have worked together to bring the publication up to date.

We're grateful to all map and guide users who have kept us informed with changes and new information they've encountered 'in the field' while using our La Palma publications. Such input is highly prized - thank you.

This third edition includes favourite routes that have been checked for accuracy and changes; there are also three new routes newly researched by Jan; Walk 35 Santa Cruz to Mirador de la Concepción; Ruta de los Molinos, Walk 36 El Paso to San Pedro via Cumbre Nueva and Walk 37 Velhoco to Cumbre.

The book includes a wide range of routes, from a handful of short routes up to 2 hours long to the longest requiring approximately 6 hours to complete. There are routes rated in difficulty from 2 walker (easy) up to 5 walker (strenuous). Mapping is fully updated and adapted from the latest edition of La Palma Tour & Trail Super-Durable Map.

The steepest island in the world, the deepest crater, the clearest skies; volcanoes you can climb without being shot into orbit; a subtropical forest minus the slimy things slinking up your trouser leg; black beaches, blue seas, high mountains, vegetation that is literally flamboyant, everything linked by over a thousand kilometres of waymarked paths; and all virtually untouched by tourism. If this sounds divine or like some lost paradise, you're not the first to think so, previous commentators having identified La Palma as the prototype for both the Elysian Fields and Atlantis! The fanciful stuff aside, the island is a walker's idyll, utterly tranquil, verdant, and almost entirely unspoiled.

Add to that a completely revised book featuring new walks, new links between established walks, and a new researcher bringing a new perspective to the island, at once confirming and consolidating the original research, and you have every reason to purchase or repurchase our guide to the delights of this most special of islands.

THE ISLAND

The Green Island or, more commonly, The Beautiful Island, La Palma is essentially a large question mark with a lot of rock draped around it. The question mark is formed by a central spine of volcanic mountains, the **Cumbre Vieja**, linked by the **Cumbre Nueva** to the loop of the **Caldera de Taburiente**, the largest water erosion crater in the world.

Walk 7 Cumbre Vieja: Pico Birigoyo

The north is wild and green, mantled in a blanket of dense forest thanks to the humidity brought by the trade winds, and so scoured with ravines that the first metalled road was only laid at the end of the twentieth century and there wasn't even a dirt track till the late fifties.

The south is a frazzled wasteland, blackened by volcanoes and thinly forested, relying largely on banana plantations and pockets of malmsey viniculture to give it a thin green fringe. Thirty-five percent of the island is officially protected, but the three most celebrated areas are the volcanoes of the **Cumbre Vieja**, the **Caldera** (literally 'cauldron') **de Taburiente**, and the **Los Tilos World Biosphere Reserve** forest.

Steepness is perhaps the defining quality of La Palma. Relative to landmass, it's the steepest island in the world and, seen from the **Cumbre Vieja** at sunset, the island's shadow reaches all the way to Tenerife, 85km away! This steepness, along with a lack of golden sands and money (apart from bananas, La Palma's principal export has been people, largely to South America, which has had a corresponding impact on local culture, cuisine and agriculture), have saved the island from mass tourism to such an extent that old black and white photos on bar walls, elsewhere an eloquent testimony to tiny fishing hamlets transformed into dense tower hamlets, might in La Palma have been taken yesterday for all that's changed.

CLIMATE & WHEN TO GO

The climate is essentially subtropical but is relieved of oppressive heat by the trade winds. Statistics suggest a very moderate year-round change in temperature, but this doesn't reflect the dramatic changes to be experienced according to shifts in altitude and cloud cover. On the north-eastern side of the island there is an almost permanent band of cloud, hovering around 1000 metres in summer and 500 metres in winter.

All the walks are possible in hot weather, though it's best to finish by midday. Most walkers come in winter, a preference reflected in the availability of direct flights, but bear in mind that temperatures at the highest point of the island can drop to zero at this time of year. Regardless of temperature, cover up in high places, where the sun is always intense.

GETTING THERE, GETTING ABOUT, GETTING A BED

In the cutthroat business of budget airlines, unprofitable services are axed and timetables changed with ruthless efficiency, so printed information is rarely valid for more than a season. There may be flights to **Santa Cruz de la Palma** from Bristol, Birmingham, Manchester, Gatwick, and Glasgow and other UK airports; check online for availability. There is also a ferry service from Tenerife, which is accessible throughout the year by a host of budget companies.

Hire-car is the simplest way of getting about. There are several agencies at the airport and every second shop in **Santa Cruz**, the capital and ferry port, seems to offer its own rental service.

Two thirds of our itineraries are accessible by bus, though the service on some lines is limited (especially at weekends) and certain roads are so winding you might not feel like walking after being swirled about in a bus.

Taxi drivers are used to dropping people off and picking them up again at the start and finish of more popular routes, though this is a comparatively expensive option.

Outside **Santa Cruz** and the few small beach resorts, single room accommodation is scarce, but there's a good spread of **Casas Rurales** available for weekly rental.

There is a fully-equipped campsite at **Laguna de Barlovento**, partially equipped camping areas at **San Antonio**, inside the **Caldera** (1 night only) and at **El Pilar** (up to 7 nights), the last two requiring a permit, free on request from the **El Paso Centro de Visitantes**; **Fuencaliente** football pitch also doubles as a camping area.

WHAT'S IN A NAME?

One surprising aspect of La Palma is that for many years nobody could decide what to call anything, so that bus lines, road numbers, villages and valleys seemed to be passing themselves off under a variety of identities. Nowadays there does seem to be more general agreement about what number bus follows what number road, but place names may still vary. Many towns have two names, for example **Breña Alta** is **San Pedro**, **Fuencaliente** is **Los Canarios**, and **Garafía** is **Santo Domingo**: this is not some cunning ruse conjured up by the locals to confuse foreigners, but a reflection of discrete village names within a larger administrative district; for example, **Santo Domingo** is the central village of the **Garafía** area. *Barrancos* or ravines (even if you don't speak Spanish, this is one word you'll never forget after a visit to La Palma) are also confusing, often boasting three distinct names from top to bottom of the same ravine. It's true, they are very big, but three names can seem excessive. Bear this in mind if you see a **Barranco del Agua** or **de los Gomeros**, **a Las Tricias**, or **a Volcán San Juan** signposted somewhere it ought not to be.

THE WALKS

A lot of time, thought and energy have been invested in waymarking a bewildering selection of paths on La Palma. However, few paths are practical in their entirety as single day excursions and, if so, are not necessarily desirable, either because they climb to places otherwise accessible by road or descend from places inaccessible by public transport. We have tried to avoid routes climbing to a point one can reach by road and have aimed for as many circuits as possible. That said, there are more linear walks than is customary in our publications, but on the steepest island in the world you either go linear or go barmy.

There are itineraries to suit all tastes and capacities, covering all the classics plus a few original routes that don't feature in conventional guidebooks. All the walks are walks and require no special expertise, though due to the island's steepness some itineraries are inevitably vertiginous, notably those following canalisation pipes, which can be very dangerous and are only recommended for experienced walkers. Where relevant, the risk of vertigo is specified in the itinerary introduction.

You will occasionally see references to controlled-skidding when descending through *picón*, the volcanic grit encountered on many walks in the south. Don't be alarmed by this. It's not a new folly dreamed up by the Dangerous Sports club but the inevitable consequence of steep slopes and deep grit. The trick is to get your heels stuck in and try not to stand on any large rocks. Apart from that, grit and gravity take care of the rest. Pure child's play!

On the whole, access is not a problem, though there are certain restrictions on access to the interior of the Caldera: large groups must have a guide and, on hot and windy days when there's a risk of fire, no more than 100 people can enter the crater.

Within each section, the first walk is suitable as a test walk for the first day and the second walk is a slightly more ambitious itinerary for the second day. The remaining walks are arranged in a vaguely geographical order, not according to difficulty or length. The last section (Walks 35-37) features itineraries that are entirely new, as opposed to those that have merely been revised or had new options incorporated.

Timings are all 'pure' timings excluding snacking, snapping and simply standing still staring. It's highly unlikely you will complete any of these walks in exactly the time specified. Try one of the shorter walks first to see how your times compare to ours. As a rule of thumb, add fifteen minutes to every timed hour. But above all, take YOUR time. There's nothing more frustrating than trying to walk at somebody else's pace, be it slower or faster than yours. All global timings include the return unless otherwise specified. Given the island's steepness, driving to the top is an ear-battering experience; you may wish to add twenty minutes to walks round the rim of the Caldera for acclimatising.

The paths are generally good and reasonably well waymarked, though signposts are occasionally vandalised. Given the quality of the waymarking, the descriptions are relatively simple. We have tried to give enough detail for those who need confirmation they're on the right path, but not so much as to irritate more confidant pathfinders with superfluity.

Walk 10: views to Volcán San Antonio

Italics are used for discrete Spanish words, also shown in purple where mentioned in the glossary at the back of the book. Place names written on signposts are contained within single quotation marks. Bold text is used for street names and place names you may need to show a bus driver if you don't want to end up at the terminal looking foolish. Consistency rather than deficient vocabulary accounts for all climbs being 'gentle', 'steady', or 'steep'.

EQUIPMENT

Unless specified in individual itineraries, nothing out of the ordinary is required, just the customary mountain-walking gear. On the whole you won't have any nasty, unseasonal surprises, but should still carry a windcheater on fine days, and always cover up from the sun when on the high peaks (hat, sunglasses, long-sleeves, suncream etc). Walking boots are preferable to sports shoes, and are essential on the high peaks where it's all rough rock and insidious grit. If you're used to walking poles you'll be glad of them here given the steepness of the island.

RISKS

Rockslides inside the **Caldera** and forest fires everywhere are a danger in summer, and there's a small risk of flash floods in the barrancos during winter, notably in the **Barranco de las Angustias**. If in doubt, ask the park authorities.

The most common problems are strong winds on the crests, mists in the north, and dehydration. Take half a litre of water per person per hour (springs may be dry in summer) and bear in mind that dehydration affects the entire body, including joints and tendons. If you suspect your knees might come in handy in thirty years' time, drink plenty before descending.

Swimming is dangerous, the undertow is strong, people drown. But then nothing so trivial as mortality ever prevented people having fun and everybody swims, despite the dire warnings of the lady in the Tourist Office. Common sense should prevail. Only swim when the sea is calm and you see other people getting in and, preferably, getting out. In high seas even the semi-natural rock pools at **Charco Azul** and **La Fajana** are not secure.

FLORA & FAUNA

This is not an exhaustive guide, but a resumé of what we noticed and learned in the course of researching the walks.

Monteverde (green-mountain) is the local name for the dense laurel, wax-myrtle, and heath tree forests (also known as *laurisilva*) that cover the northern, north-eastern, and eastern slopes of the island. In the text, I use *laurisilva* in a loose, generic sense, though inevitably the flora, even of superficially similar woodland, is more complex than this suggests. In drier areas the correct term is *fayal-brezal*, a composite of the Spanish words for wax-myrtle and tree-heath.

At lower altitudes, the *laurisilva* is interspersed with chestnut and the occasional walnut. At higher altitudes and in the north-west, Canary Pine dominate though there are some Canary Cedar, too. Along the coast, palms are sufficiently prevalent to be used as brooms by street cleaners.

Another characteristic tree is the *drago* or Dragon Tree, a survivor, like the *laurisilva*, of the last Ice Age, and weird enough to have featured in Hieronymous Bosch's 'Garden of Delights'. You will also see eucalyptus, pepper trees, flamboyants, avocado, fig, orange, apple and pear trees, the last five often run wild.

Of flowers and shrubs, look out for rock rose, dog rose, houseleeks, viper's bugloss, violets, gladioli, forget-me-nots, hydrangea, taginaste, cistus and broom, according to altitude, season and orientation.

Prickly pear, as elsewhere in Spain, were long the commonplace alternative to a septic tank and every tiny country cottage (and they are all very tiny) will have its patch to process the household waste. This useful plant not only provided fruit and plumbing, but played host to a flaky white parasite (in evidence on several of our walks) from which cochineal was extracted, a lucrative business before it was superseded by synthetic dyes.

Otherwise, man's biggest impact has been the development of mass banana plantations, which cover the coastal areas, like a sombre green blanket, only broken up by rough riddled walls erected as windbreaks.

Though the **Caldera de Taburiente** park leaflet claims 25 recorded bird species, I can't pretend to have seen anything like that variety myself. Kestrels, chaffinch and rock-doves are common, but perhaps the most emblematic and endearing bird on the island is the chough, with its brilliant orange bill and bright stockinged legs. The sight of a parliament of choughs, chuntering about, chattering and pecking at the ground, like a charabanc party on an outing, is always diverting.

Apart from an inordinate number of dead rats squashed on the road and hordes of diminutive rabbits nervously darting all over the place (with good cause given the gangs of hunters out every weekend with their packs of friendly hunting dogs), the terrestrial fauna is limited. We saw one *mouflon* and that was about it. Ubiquitous, however, is the blue-jowled Canary-lizard. These are the source of the constant rustling in the leaves as you walk along woodland paths. Though frightened of walkers, they are fascinated by picnickers and can become alarmingly inquisitive.

Entomologists will delight in the butterflies which, like the shrubs, attain tropical proportions, and in the tremendous number of dragon flies.

To find out more about the island's flora and fauna, you should visit the **Parque Botánico y Faunístico Maroparque** in **Breña Alta** and the **Parque Paraíso de las Aves** (Paradise Park for Birdlife) in **El Paso**.

EATING & DRINKING

With plenty of good country restaurants, strong local wines, and shady pine forests, this is the land of a thousand siestas. Imagining a typical meal, you might care to slake your thirst with one of the local beers (*cerveza*), Dorada, Reina, and Tropical, all of which are additive free and, by Spanish standards, excellent.

These might be accompanied by a delicious grilled goat cheese (*queso asado*) brushed with green pepper and/or coriander sauce, *mojo verde*, the classic Canaries sauce that goes well with everything savoury.

Vegetarians will then have to hope there's something based on chick-peas (*garbanzas*), beans (*judias*), or lentils (*lentejas*) without too much meat floating about in it. Otherwise you'll be stuck with the standard salad (*ensalada mixta*), omelette (*tortilla*) and more goat's cheese, unless you're a fish-eater, in which case you could try the local chowder (*sopa de arroz*), or one of the many fish (*pescado*) that are either unique to these waters or uniquely named.

Apart from the ubiquitous bream (*dorada*) and hake (*merluza* aka *cherne*), the former farmed the latter wild, few of the local fish will be familiar, but nothing will be quite so strange as Tollos a la Canaria. Don't worry if this challenges your Spanish; it challenges the Spanish of mainland Spaniards, too! It's the local word for shark (*tiburón* in Spanish) and once you've tasted it (strong and very fishy), you may begin to appreciate why they took the trouble to rename it.

On the whole though, main courses are meat (*carne*) - and very good, too. Nearly everything is raised and fed naturally on the island, so you won't find yourself confronted with a shrivelled lump of leather swimming in a puddle of water, hormones, and antibiotics. Even the beef (*ternera*, *buey*, or *res*), a variety of elderly veal on the mainland, is excellent. But the real specialities are roasted kid (*cabrito*), stewed goat (*cabra con salsa*), rabbit (*conejo*), pork loin and chops (respectively *solomillo* and *chuletas de cerdo*), and to a lesser extent lamb (*cordero*).

Anything that's not stewed will preferably be grilled on an open fire (*a la brasa*) and will undoubtedly be served with more mojo, this time *mojo rojo* made with red peppers, and the excellent local potatoes, *papas arrugadas*, or 'wrinkled potatoes', boiled in their jackets in sea water or with lots of salt and little water, resulting in a taste and texture that suggests parboiling and baking. A popular and filling snack introduced by migrants returning from Venezuela are *arepas*, thick maize pancakes wrapped round a savoury filling.

By now you will doubtless be getting thirsty again. In small country restaurants, it's generally worthwhile trying the house wine, *vino de la casa*, which won't be a fine wine, but will be an experience, usually pleasurable. Red wines tend to be light on colour and heavy on everything else. The best of the reds is Teneguia Negramoll, *negramoll* being one of the island's key grape varieties.

Tea wines are not a remote echo of the temperance movement, but wines matured in barrels made from the heartwood of the Canary pine, also known as tea, which gives them a distinctively resinous aftertaste (tea is also the wood used for the balconies of traditional La Palman town houses). They're often compared to retsina, but might better be described as a dry Madeira laced with thyme. Peculiar, but pleasant.

The white wines are light and fruity and worth trying. The most famous local wine is Malvasia, better known in English as Malmsey, a sweet, pleasantly light dessert wine. A dry variety can be found, but isn't worth the search.

Wherever possible, walks end at or near a *típico*, a rated bar or restaurant.

OTHER THINGS TO SEE AND DO

La Palma is refreshingly free of the usual tourist circus, but there's plenty to fill a day off walking.

Even if you're relying on buses for most of your trip, we recommend hiring a car for a day or two, as driving round the island gives a different perspective on the place, usually enjoyable, sometimes alarming, notably on minor roads down to the coast. If you do go on a car tour, it's worth visiting the *piscinas naturales*, or 'natural' swimming pools at **La Fajana** and **Charco Azul**, below **Barlovento** and **Los Sauces**, always bearing in mind the warning about swimming.

The islanders are very proud of their petroglyphs, commonly whorled but occasionally rectilinear symbols carved onto rocks by the pre-hispanic inhabitants, the Auaritas (often called Benahoare, the island's original name, meaning Land of my Ancestors). There's disagreement about what these carvings mean, some claiming religious symbolism, others the location of springs. On the whole, they're not the most stunning archaeological finds, but evocative enough if you happen to stumble on one in the wild. Most tourists see them in the **Belmaco Cave** or **Parque Cultural La Zarza**.

The Tourist Information Office can provide up-to-date information about *fiestas*, fishing trips, whale watching excursions, horse-riding, and the numerous adventure sports the island has to offer, notably diving, climbing, pot-holing, paragliding, and mountain-biking. The scuba diving is particulary interesting off the shores near **Fuencaliente** thanks to the 1972 volcanic eruption centred on **Teneguía**. The volcanic activity also means that La Palma is a haven for caving. The island's best known cave is **Todoque**. It is also one of the longest and features unusual endemic fauna. Alternatively, if you want something a little more extraterrestrial, a visit to the Observatory at **Roque de Los Muchachos** can be arranged.

There's a good fresh produce market (*mercado*) from Mondays to Saturdays, 06.00 - 14.30 in **Santa Cruz de La Palma**, and in **Los Llanos de Aridane** with similar opening hours, and also in **Mazo** on Saturdays and Sundays. Otherwise, to see something a bit different, it's worth visiting the *Mercadillo* on Saturday afternoons and Sundays (11.00 - 15.00) at **Puntagorda**, where local artisans and smallholders sell their wares and produce.

It's also worth taking a day to wander around **Santa Cruz de la Palma**. The Tourist Information Office booklet, 'A Historical and Artistic Guide to Santa Cruz de la Palma' is a good starting point for exploring the cobbled streets of this quaint and attractive little town. There are plenty of places to stop and take in the architecture and atmosphere over a *cortado* or *cerveza*, and several of the town's most historic buildings are open to the public, some housing museums.

The wooden balconies seen on many of the older properties are built onto the rear of the buildings. Some of the most photographed are those found facing the sea, their front doors opening onto **Calle O'Daly**.

Strolling round the charming old town, you're bound to see somebody hand-rolling cigars - and probably smoking a Marlboro at the same time. The tobacco industry is in decline, but La Palman cigars have been compared not unfavourably with their Cuban model.

Most of the town's traditional shops are to be found around **Calle O'Daly** and the narrow streets leading off it. If you enjoy searching out unusual keepsakes, this is the place to head for.

But, of course, by far the best souvenir you'll bring back from your stay on the island is a headful of memories of magnificent scenery, spectacular views, and wonderful paths. So get those boots on and let's go!

DWG's Symbols Rating Bar shows key information about a walking route in a quick glance. Remember that effort/exertion and refreshment ratings are the author's opinion and the time shown is walking time without stops.

our rating for effort/exertion:

1 very easy **4** energetic
2 easy   **5** strenuous
3 average

approximate **time** to complete a walk (compare your times against ours early in a walk) - does not include stopping time

approximate walking **distance** in kilometres

200m

850m

approximate **ascents/descents** in metres (N = negligible)

linear route, out & back

linear route, one way

circular route

figure of eight route

risk of **vertigo** from:
1= some risk to **3**=high risk

refreshments
(may be at start or end of a route only)

Notes on the text

Place names are shown in **bold text**, except where we refer to a written sign, when they are enclosed in single quotation marks. Local or unusual words are shown in *italics*, and are explained in the accompanying text.

Walk descriptions include:

- timing in minutes, shown as (40M)
- compass directions, shown as (NW)
- heights in metres, shown as (1355m)
- GPS waypoints, shown as (Wp.3)

A Note About Walking Times

Walking times create more discussion than any other aspect of walking guide books. Our walking times are for ***continuous walking*** at an easy pace without stops, representing the quickest time you are likely to complete a route. Most of us walk at a similar pace; approx 4-6kmh. As our routes are planned as fun adventures you are unlikely to simply march along the route from start to finish. We all take stops to enjoy the views, marvel at the flora, or simply to take a break. As a result, time taken will be longer than the 'continuous walking' time so we suggest you add 25-50% to those times, to allow for the stops you'll make along the route.

WALK LOCATOR MAP

MAP PROVENANCE

Simplified and adapted map data provided by **Discovery Walking Guides Ltd**. (copyright David Brawn) has been used to prepare this locator map.

The latest edition of **La Palma** **Tour & Trail Super-Durable Map** is available from booksellers. Digital mapping for a variety of destinations including La Palma is available from:

www.dwgwalking.co.uk

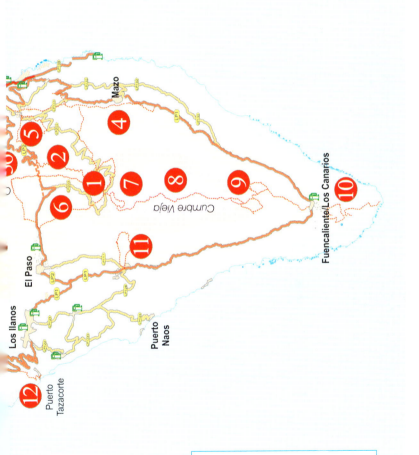

Please Note:

This locator map is intended to give a general indication of each walk area.

The map sections in this book have been adapted from **La Palma Super-Durable Tour & Trail Map** published by **Discovery Walking Guides Ltd.**

La Palma Tour & Trail Legend

ALTITUDE

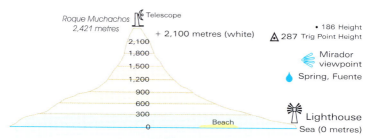

Roque Muchachos
2,421 metres

Telescope

+ 2,100 metres (white)

2,100
1,800
1,500
1,200
900
600
300
0

Beach

• 186 Height

△ 287 Trig Point Height

Mirador viewpoint

Spring, Fuente

Lighthouse

Sea (0 metres)

ROADS

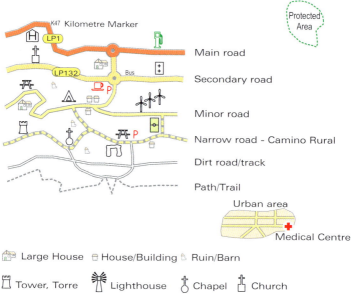

K47 Kilometre Marker

LP1

Protected Area

Main road

LP132   Bus

Secondary road

P

Minor road

P

Narrow road - Camino Rural

Dirt road/track

Path/Trail

Urban area

Medical Centre

 Large House House/Building Ruin/Barn

 Tower, Torre Lighthouse Chapel Church

 P Parking Bar/Rest Hotel Petrol Picnic area

Sports Ground Bus Bus Stop Camping Cemetery

Wind Turbine Historical Site Information Office

Walking Routes

Walk! La Palma Route (Red) 17

GR (Gran Recorrido) & PR (Pequeño Recorrido)

GR130

GR130 - Gran Recorrido
PRLP12 - Pequeño Recorrido

PRLP12

USING GPS ON LA PALMA

All the routes* in this book have been recorded by GPS and are accurately described, so adventuring on our routes is simply a matter of following the walk description. *Note that GPS reception is unreliable once you have left the start of Walk 25 and Walk 26, on these 'barranco' routes use the walk descriptions for your navigation.

A GPS is not necessary but is very useful if you want to know exactly where you are on a walking route. If it's your first time on La Palma then a GPS will be useful in finding the start of each walking route; with the walking route's waypoints loaded in your GPS, simply activate the 'Go To' function for Waypoint 1 of your chosen walk route.

All the waypoints for our La Palma walking routes are available as a free downloadable zip file. Locate the download page on our website, then download the zip file to your hard drive, unzip the file and you will have all the individual waypoint files in gpx file format; then simply load the files you want into your GPS or phone app.

If you are thinking of a GPS for your walking navigation, then our GPS The Easy Way introduction to GPS walking navigation is available as a free download in pdf format from DWG's website:- www.dwgwalking.co.uk

3/4G phone users should look at the GPS apps by MyTrails and Viewranger who supply digital editions of our Tour & Trail Maps for their apps which enables you to use your phone offline as a full mapping GPS unit without incurring any phone call or roaming charges. For more information see their websites.

Discovery Walking Guides publish Custom Map digital editions of Tour & Trail Maps in kmz file format for use in Google Earth and with the Custom Maps function of Garmin mapping GPS units such as eTrex20/30, Oregon, Dakota, Montana. See DWG's website:- www.dwgwalking.co.uk for information.

1 MONTEVERDE: PARED VIEJA - EL PILAR

An ideal introduction to the flora of the *monteverde* or 'green mountain', the local name for the jungle-like *laurisilva* forests of the highlands. Following mostly waymarked trails, we climb through classic *monteverde* to the pine fringed spine of the island, the **Cumbre Nueva**, then return to the popular **Pared Vieja** *área recreativa* via a lovely donkey trail.

3 | 2H | 6.5 km | 275m / 275m | ↻ | 0

Access by car or taxi
The walk starts from the **Pared Vieja Área Recreativa** at km10.9 of the **LP-301** between **San Isidro** and **El Pilar.** Park in the *área recreativa* car-park, 40 metres west of the entrance to **Pared Vieja.**

Our start at Wp.1

Our itinerary begins opposite the entrance to the **Pared Vieja** *área recreativa* beside a signpost for the **PR-18** (Wp.1 0M). Ignoring a path to the left, we take the dirt track on the right, the waymarked **SL-132** which winds through the woods for a kilometre**.**

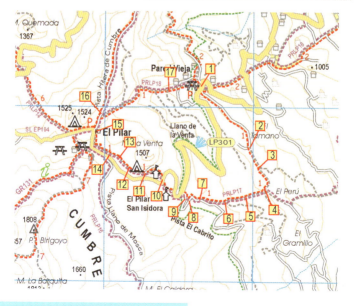

When the track swings right for 'Camino de la Faya' and 'Refugio El Pilar' (Wp.2 15M), we turn left, leaving the **SL-132**.

At a Y-junction (Wp.3 20M), we ignore a green-gated track to the left and take the barred track to the right, climbing across abandoned terraces with fine views along the coast and over to Tenerife. The track becomes increasingly overgrown as it approaches a T-junction with a clear dirt track, where we turn left then, almost immediately, right, joining the **PR-17** (Wp.4 30M) (currently very poorly waymarked, though hopefully this will be remedied with time). Ignoring three branches to the left, we follow the infrequent yellow-and-white waymarks of the PR, climbing steadily to steeply.

After crossing a dirt track and passing a small white cross, we reach a signposted junction with the **SL-124** and **SL-132** (Wp.5 40M), where we carry straight on.

Views of Cumbre Nueva after Wp.5

Turning right at the junction with the **Pista Camino de la Faya** (Wp.6 45M), we continue climbing, passing a *mirador* with an explanatory picture-board about the *monteverde*.

After a large bungalow, we bear right (Wp.7 50M) on the dusty **Pista General** or **Pista El Cabrito**, which runs along the eastern flank of the **Cumbre Vieja**. Crossing a wooden footbridge (Wp.8 53M), we climb steeply on a narrow, shady, shortcut path before rejoining the dirt track (Wp.9 55M).

Fifteen metres to the right we leave the track again, turning left to continue on our shady path as it runs parallel to the road, again climbing steeply before levelling off as the *monteverde* merges with pine.

Crossing the road (Wp.10 60M), we continue through dense woods, passing a picture-board about the *faya* or wax-myrtle. After another brief climb, the path levels out and becomes a broad walking trail meandering through the pine, crossing a dirt track (Wp.11 65M) and a gully (Wp.12 67M). Bearing left up (a minor) forestry track, the **Pista Hoyo de Rehielo**, we ignore a branch to the left and cross another gully (Wp.13 70M) onto another path that soon joins the road (Wp.14 73M).

After passing an adventure park and following the road through a long bend, we bear right at a signpost onto a broad dirt track, the **Pista Hilera** (Wp.15 80M), 200 metres above the **Pilar Refuge** and camping area. Ten metres behind the 'Comienzo Municipio Breña Alta' panel, we bear right on a narrow path, signposted 'PR-18' and 'GR-131', descending through the woodland.

We follow the **PR-18** all the way back to our starting point. The path, which to begin with is slippery with pine needles, comes to a signposted junction (Wp.16 83M) where we bear right, leaving the **GR-131**.

Laurisilva **between Wps. 16 & 17**

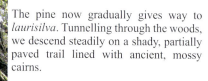

The pine now gradually gives way to *laurisilva*. Tunnelling through the woods, we descend steadily on a shady, partially paved trail lined with ancient, mossy cairns.

Emerging from the tree cover, we traverse large blocks of rock to a junction with a dirt track below a small shrine (Wp.17 105M). Crossing the track, we follow a clearly waymarked path down to Wp.1.

The small shrine at Wp.17

A long, easy walk serving as an excellent introduction to the flora of La Palma and the local transport system. Snaking along below the **Cumbre Nueva**, we pass through dense *laurisilva* to the **Pared Vieja Área Recreativa**, set amid fine Canary pine. En route we see shrubs the size of bushes, bushes the size of trees, and get a slightly gamey whiff of decaying vegetation reminiscent of the forests of West Africa. Descending on one of the old donkey trails that were once the only land link between the two sides of the island, we cross largely abandoned farmland with fine views of the countryside south of **Santa Cruz**. There are so many junctions that the descent sounds confusing, but the waymarking is adequate and the route fairly obvious on the ground.

3 | 3H 20M | 15.5 km | 50m / 900m | one way | 3*

* in San José

Access by bus:
N° 300 from **Santa Cruz** (NB the bus from **Los Llanos** uses the newer lower tunnel). Ask for **Túnel de la Cumbre** and, if any doubt is expressed, **Pista de los Lomos à Pared Vieja**. This should be an official stop, though the signboard is missing.

The walk starts in front of the tunnel at km15.5 of the **LP-3**, on a tarmac track heading south between a green electricity substation and a signboard for 'Parque Natural Cumbre Vieja' (Wp.1 0M). The tarmac gives way to dirt after fifty metres and we climb gently, passing a number of secluded (and frequently litter strewn) spots. Fortunately, the detritus doesn't last long and we are soon surrounded by lush vegetation.

The tunnel and signboard at Wp.1

The track levels off below shallow cliffs capped with masses of laurel (Wp.2 15M) and, at the next bend (Wp.3 20M), we see Tenerife and La Gomera. Shortly after a rockspill with a pair of rough boulder 'stools' (Wp.4 30M), we pass a sheer cliff (Wp.5 33M) and climb very slightly, winding into a gully packed with towering laurel and carpeted with dead leaves (Wp.6 45M). Passing a second rockspill, distinguished by the stump of a fallen tree (Wp.7 65M), we again climb very slightly to an exposed stretch in sight of the northernmost volcanoes on the **Cumbre Vieja** (Wp.8 80M) (see Walks 7&8). The laurel gives way to Canary pine as we approach **Pared Vieja**, where we pass to the left of the first building (Wp.9 90M) and cross the car-park to the road (Wp.10).

Opposite the entrance to the *área recreativa*, we take a broad partially paved trail marked by a 'PR-18' sign, descending to re-cross the road a couple of minutes later (Wp.11 95M). Bearing right at a Y-junction, we cross the road once more (Wp.12 105M) and traverse open farmland.

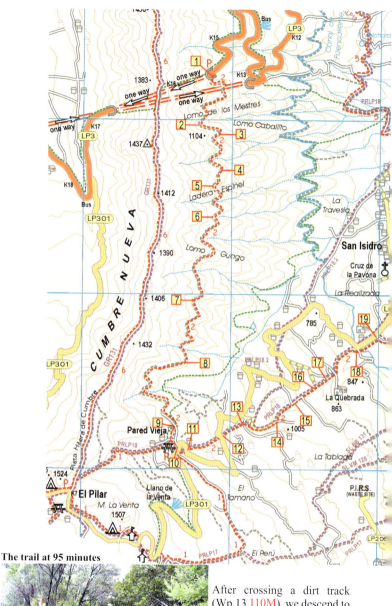

The trail at 95 minutes

After crossing a dirt track (Wp.13 110M), we descend to a tarmac lane where the **PR-18.2** bears left for 'El Llanito' and we turn right for 'Los Guinchos'. When the tarmac lane becomes a dirt track (Wp.14 120M), we bear left (NE), recovering the old trail and resuming our steady descent.

Joining a narrow, partially overgrown track, we bear right, descending to a concrete track (Wp.15 125M). Bearing right again, we maintain direction (NE) for fifty metres down to a staggered crossroads. Immediately after the first left-hand branch, we turn left on a waymarked path, briefly recovering the donkey trail before passing a small green house (Wp.16 130M), where concrete resumes.

Ten metres before the concrete gives way to tarmac, we bear right (Wp.17 135M), recovering the donkey trail and descending, first towards a small green pylon, then between retaining walls toward a large farm backed by a paddock shaded by large chestnut trees.

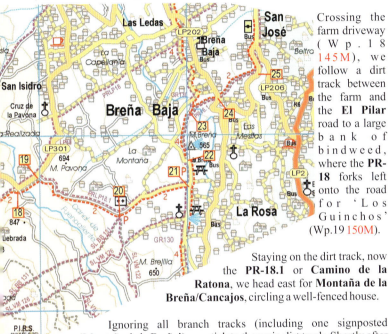

Crossing the farm driveway (Wp.18 145M), we follow a dirt track between the farm and the **El Pilar** road to a large bank of bindweed, where the **PR-18** forks left onto the road for 'Los Guinchos' (Wp.19 150M).

Staying on the dirt track, now the **PR-18.1** or **Camino de la Ratona**, we head east for **Montaña de la Breña/Cancajos**, circling a well-fenced house.

Ignoring all branch tracks (including one signposted 'Montaña de la Breña'), we stick to the main dirt track. Shortly after glimpsing a garden of remembrance on our left, we turn left at a T-junction (Wp.20 170M), descending to the cemetery car-park.

Following the cemetery road down to a T-junction, we turn left on the **GR-130** (Wp.21 180M), passing an *área recreativa*, fifty metres after which, the road climbs to **Montaña de la Breña** and we fork left on a GR-signposted walking trail (Wp.22 185M). The trail runs into a dirt track descending to a junction (Wp.23 190M) where the **GR-130** continues in a northerly direction and we bear right for **Cancajos**. Our narrow path soon crosses the **Canal del Estado**, then descends to the **San Pedro** road (Wp.24 195M). Fifty metres to the north, just after house N°90, we turn right on a broad 'Pista Privada' concrete track. After climbing briefly, the track descends between houses and dwindles to a narrow dirt path, briefly interrupted by a thirty metre stretch of concrete track before reaching the **San José** road (Wp.25 205M). Bearing left, we follow the road into **San José**, for refreshments and bus N°200 back to **Santa Cruz**.

On the official map of La Palma's paths, the **PR-2.3** looks like nothing much at all. Don't be deceived. This is very much 'something', far and away the most adventurous and riskiest walk in the book. The **Barranco de la Madera** is a bit grim at the beginning, dry, dusty, degraded and dispiriting, but as we climb, the walls of the ravine rise above us, the silence deepens, and we are suffused with a growing sense of isolation, the uncanny hush broken only by the occasional bird, the only other walker, a disgruntled mouflon disdainfully stalking away up an almost vertical cliff. Then, just when it seems things can't get any wilder, we reach our sensational return route, following the **Galería de la Madera**, channelling water through a series of tunnels down to **Santa Cruz**. And it all starts a short bus ride from the town centre at one of the island's top tourist attractions, the seventeenth century **Santuario de las Nieves**.

So why isn't it thronged with walkers? The reason is simple: between the tunnels we teeter along a narrow canal path above sheer drops. It is VERY vertiginous, potentially dangerous, and should NOT be undertaken by the inexperienced or those who dislike heights. DO NOT do this walk alone or when it's wet underfoot. A pocket torch is useful, but not indispensable. NB Between waypoints 5 and 9 GPS reception can be very erratic and should not be relied upon for this section of the route.

* at the Santuario de las Nieves bar

Access by car and bus:
Bus Nº L303. If possible, park in the shady alley behind the Sanctuary. Otherwise there's ample parking in the car-park just above it.

We start from the **Sanctuary Plaza de las Nieves** (Wp.1 0M) on a stone stairway in front of the **Bar/Restaurante Parilla las Nieves**.

Santuario de las Nieves - the start at Wp.1

The stairs run into a cobbled alley descending to the sanctuary access road, at the bottom of which, we cross the main road just north of a tunnel. Bearing right toward a breeze-block cabin, we take a dusty dirt track up the left bank of the **Barranco de la Madera**.

Climbing steadily, we cross the watercourse (Wp.2 10M), after which the track becomes stonier and less dusty. The *barranco* narrows as we continue to climb, getting deeper and stiller, the silence gradually intensifying after the second of two aqueducts (Wp.3 20M). Entering the 'Parque Natural las Nieves' (Wp.4 35M), we cross the **Canal del Estado**, and the ravine closes around us, ever tighter and more spectacular. The track occasionally levels off, but generally climbs steadily or steeply. After zigzagging past a small ruin (Wp.5 65M), we reach a goatherd's cabin and the end of the dirt track (Wp.6 70M).

Continuing on a broad path following the **Galería Mercedes** canalisation pipe, we climb into the depths of the *barranco*, where apart from the occasional roar of water, the silence is absolute - also absolute is the absence of satellite coverage for GPS, hence no waypoints. Like the track before it, the path levels off occasionally, but on the whole, climbs steadily, passing a slightly vertiginous stretch under an overhang. After the third level stretch, we pass through a rock archway (90M) leading to another slightly vertiginous section. A fourth level stretch leads to the mouth of a deep tunnel (100M) (a delightfully fresh bolt-hole in hot weather) littered with mining trolley-cars and rails.

We have now reached the last part of our climb. Taking a steep, slippery path to the right of the tunnel, we leave the **Galería Mercedes** and, thirty metres later, cross back onto the left bank of the *barranco*. The path here is rougher and slightly overgrown, but always visible and well waymarked, as it climbs steeply to what appears to be an impenetrable wall of rock. Had it not been for the engineers, it would have been!

Pressing on, always climbing, always heading west up the *barranco* (there's nowhere else to go) we finally come to the foot of a huge dry waterfall.

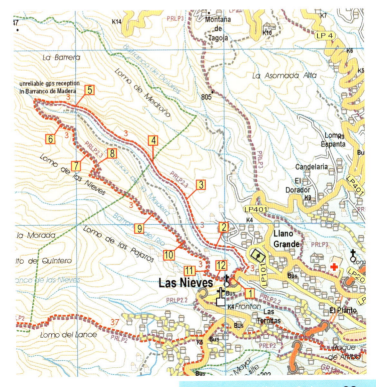

There's a small stone bridge to the right and, on our left, the first tunnel along the *galería* (120M). This is where sufferers of vertigo have to decide how badly they want to do the full loop. The worst sections come after the first (a narrow path with an inconveniently bulging wall) and second (a long narrow stretch over sheer drops) tunnels.

At first, the tunnel looks dismal, but after a few metres a 'window' brightens the way. Crouching low, we creep along, eventually emerging on the first very vertiginous stretch (130M), which is mercifully short, only lasting some 75 metres before we get to the second tunnel. The path after the second tunnel (135M) is narrower, but marginally less vertiginous thanks to shrubbery and trees, which act as 'blinkers' shielding us from the drop. The third tunnel (Wp.7 140M) is only a few metres long.

We now reach more densely wooded land and, though there are one or two vertiginous stretches, the worst is over. If you've coped so far, there's nothing much to worry about anymore, apart from braining yourself in the fourth tunnel (Wp.8 150M), where the roof occasionally dips down unexpectedly. A final stroll through an alley of laurel (Wp.9 160M) leads to a large water tower (Wp.10 170M) where our descent begins.

Briefly bearing left, away from the water pipe, we zigzag down to rejoin it a little way below. One hundred metres later (Wp.11 175M), another zigzagging path takes us away from the *galería* (S) onto the **Lomo de las Nieves**, which divides the **Barrancos de la Madera** and **de las Nieves**. From here, the major part of the descent is straightforward as we follow a steep path down through the pine, largely on the southern side of the spur with steadily improving views of the countryside behind **Santa Cruz**. The only slightly confusing point is when the path swings left, back towards **Barranco de la Madera**, and an old, faded cross indicates we leave the main path and take a faint branch to the right (Wp.12 200M). Ignore the cross and stay on the main path. Soon after this we see the **Mirca** sports stadium.

Ignoring two minor branches up the **Barranco de las Nieves**, we follow a galería for 75 metres before bearing right (SE) (Wp.13 220M) to continue our steady descent. Passing a house with a large pond/reservoir and a garden packed with palm trees, we emerge on a small plateau, where we bear right on a grassy path passing between two small ruins. Crossing a concrete track (Wp.14 230M), we bear left on a broad dirt trail down to a dry reservoir (Wp.15 235M) where we bear left again to descend into the large car-park immediately behind the sanctuary and our starting point.

4 THE GOOD, THE HIGH, THE LOW & THE BAD

If you're seeking wild places and dislike tarmac, read no further; there are other routes in this book for you. If, on the other hand, you want a blast of fresh air on a blustery winter's day when wild places might be a tad too wild, the **GR-130** is ideal. Starting with the 'good', **Buenavista**, we visit the 'high' and 'low' of the **Breñas Alta** and **Baja**, then take the **PR-16.1** down to the 'bad country' of **Malpaís**.

Buenavista is home to the old airport and the **Mirador de la Concepción** overlooking **Santa Cruz**; **Breña Alta** or **San Pedro** is the nucleus of the declining cigar manufactories and boasts the island's most famous Dragon Trees, the twin **Dragos Gemelos**; **Breña Baja** or **San José** developed round the seventeenth century church of the same name, built to minister to the farming community, and is now the administrative hub of **La Palma**'s tourism industry; finally, **Malpaís**, a windswept volcanic landscape so inhospitable its hapless residents were reduced to the desperate measure of cultivating grapes for malmsey! The roads are peaceful lanes, apart from the climb past **Ermita de San Miguel**. The plethora of lanes and tracks make the route sound complicated, but the waymarking is clear, except in built up areas. The 'average' exertion rating is due to the length.

* in Malpaís

Access by bus:
N°300, 302, 303 to reach the start, and N°201 at the end. The bus stops are 100 metres north of Wp.1 and fifty metres north of Wp.24.

We start in **Buenavista Abajo** at the symbolic 'gate' of curving metal pillars perched on the raised intersection of the **Breña Alta** road and the **LP-2** to **Los Llanos** (Wp.1 0M).

If you haven't yet visited it, it's worth detouring north 100 metres to climb the **Mirador de la Concepción**.

The start at the curving 'gate'

For the main walk, we follow the **Breña Alta** road (S) and, just before a U-turn roundabout, fork left into an alley alongside the main road. Crossing a side road, we pass house N°58 on a surfaced lane, the **Camino Real**, which we follow into **San Pedro**, briefly rejoining the main road en route (Wp.2 5M). As the lane climbs into town, we maintain direction (S), passing 'Calle Espinel'.

Approaching the church, we bear left on **Calle del Cura** (Wp.3 14M) then cross the **San José** road onto **Calle Luis Wandevalle**. When this swings left, we maintain our southerly direction on a concrete then cobbled track, **Calle Cuesta La Pata**, which descends out of the urban area into **Barranco del Llanito**.

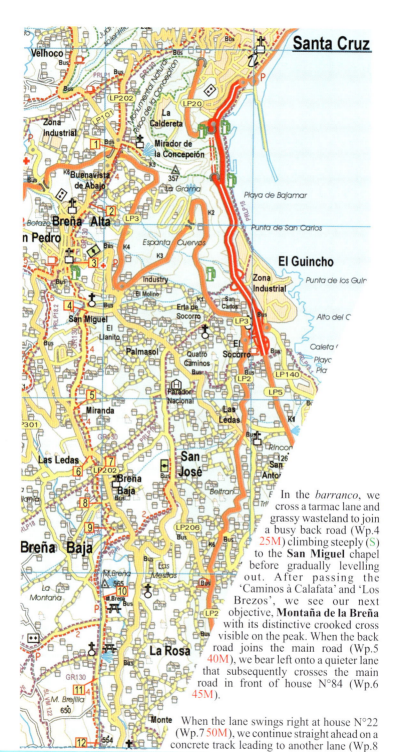

In the *barranco*, we cross a tarmac lane and grassy wasteland to join a busy back road (Wp.4 25M) climbing steeply (S) to the **San Miguel** chapel before gradually levelling out. After passing the 'Caminos à Calafata' and 'Los Brezos', we see our next objective, **Montaña de la Breña** with its distinctive crooked cross visible on the peak. When the back road joins the main road (Wp.5 40M), we bear left onto a quieter lane that subsequently crosses the main road in front of house N°84 (Wp.6 45M).

When the lane swings right at house N°22 (Wp.7 50M), we continue straight ahead on a concrete track leading to another lane (Wp.8

55M). Turning left then sharp right forty metres later, we follow a third lane to a junction beside a **Breña Baja** tourist information board. Bearing right, we climb to a Y-junction (Wp.9 60M) and fork right on a waymarked concrete track.

When the track swings right, we climb past a water-hut and clamber onto the **Canal del Estado**. Bearing left, we follow the canal round to a road and take a concrete track for **Mazo**. A short, steep climb brings us onto dirt track, where we join the **PR-18.1** (see Walk 2). Climbing the track, we pass in front of a bright orange house and continue climbing steadily on a broad dirt trail, joining **Carrer de la Montaña** below **Montaña de la Breña** (Wp.10 75M).

Maintaining direction (S), we follow **Carrer de la Montaña** past the **Montaña de la Breña Área Recreativa** and the turn off for the **PR18.1**, after which we have excellent views out to sea and along the coast.

Climbing past the 'Cuesta Anselmo' and a small *mirador*, we follow **Carrer de la Montaña** till it swings left and we continue straight ahead on a minor lane (Wp.11 90M). The lane climbs steeply for fifty metres before levelling off then climbing again and running into a partially cobbled track. The track runs between well-maintained walls, passing an idyllic little farm with a characteristically tall, wind-cheating La Palman chimney (Wp.12 100M).

Joining a narrow lane (Wp.13 105M), we cross the **PR-17** and continue on an intermittently metalled track into the outskirts of **Mazo**. When the asphalted **Camino El Poleal** swings left, we continue straight ahead on the **Camino Las Toscas** dirt track (Wp.14 120M), passing below a small *área recreativa*, immediately after which the track becomes a tarmac lane and the **PR-16** branches left into **Mazo** (Wp.15 130M). **Camino Las Toscas** eventually joins the **LP-121** (Wp.16 135M), which we follow (S) till it swings down toward the main road and we bear right for **Los Canarios**. After traversing a dry watercourse and passing behind a large reservoir, we cross a dirt track, and continue on a slightly overgrown path running along a terrace, which gradually broadens to a rough dirt track descending to a small *fuente/área recreativa* next to the main road (Wp.17 145M).

Continuing on a gently sloping lane parallel to the road, we bear left just after the second branch on the right, taking another overgrown path, also parallel to the road. The path gradually bears away from the road, climbing gently before levelling out near the straggly hamlet of **La Salina** and crossing a concrete track (Wp.18 155M). Climbing alongside a gully, we cross a lane, ten metres above which we bear left, crossing the gully onto a donkey trail leading to another tarmac lane (Wp.19 160M), on which the GR is joined by the **PR-16.1** from **Roque Niquiomo**. The two paths follow the lane until a small shrine (on our left) with a blue background and white stars (Wp.20 170M), where we turn left, leaving the GR and descending on a broad cobbled way.

The cobbled way runs into a road, which we follow till it swings left and we continue straight ahead on more cobbles. Passing under the main road to **Fuencaliente** (Wp.21 180M), we join a tiny tarmac lane and continue descending with fine views over the coast. Ten metres after the tarmac gives way to concrete, we bear right to recover the cobbled way. After a steep descent, we turn right on a minor road (Wp.22 185M), which we follow to a classic La Palman 'dalmatian' house (N°104) (Wp.23 200M) where we bear left, leaving the road to descend on a waymarked concrete then dirt track that brings us into **Malpais** next to the **Bar/Arepera Chaplin** (Wp.24 205M).

The **PR-19** is ostensibly a tour of the springs dotted about the hillside behind **Breña Alta**, but the real star of the show is the magnificent chestnut forest. Water is available en route, but best take your own, too. The itinerary is well waymarked and signposted.

* in San Pedro

Access by car:
Park at Wp.2

Access by bus:
Bus N°s 202, 300, 302, 303 run between **Santa Cruz** and our start in **San Pedro**'s main plaza..

We start from the main plaza in **San Pedro** (Wp.1 0M) opposite the post-office bus-stop and, more importantly, **Bar Teneguia** (see below).

The main square, San Pedro, our start point

Heading south on the main road, we continue on the tarmac when the pavement ends and, 150 metres later, just after a large, pink house, turn right

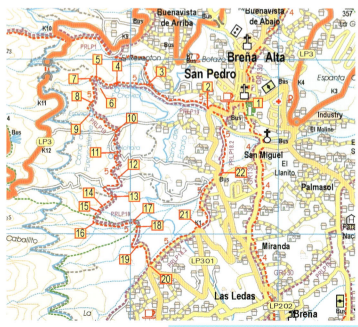

on the access road for the 'Viveros Las Breñas', descending into the **Barranco Aguasencio** (Wp.2 5M) where the **PR-19** officially starts.

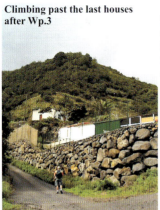

Climbing past the last houses after Wp.3

Taking the surfaced track up the *barranco*, we climb to a Y-junction (Wp.3 15M) below a house with green gates, where we bear left, climbing past the last houses onto a dirt trail.

The trail climbs steadily up the *barranco*, passing the **Fuente Chavez** (Wp.4 25M) before reaching a junction marked by a PR signpost (Wp.5 37M). The left-hand fork leads to **Fuente Grande** (Wp.6 40M), which isn't much of a *fuente* (its waters are siphoned off elsewhere), but is a pleasantly shady spot nestling below low cliffs.

For the main walk, we bear right at Wp.5 and climb steeply, passing a waypost (Wp.7 45M) and gradually bearing south into the heart of the chestnut woods. Crossing a swale beside a ruined cabin, we climb a rough earthen bank and cross a grassy dirt track (Wp.8 55M) onto the path for **El Llanito**, the signpost direction we follow for the rest of the walk.

Steep dirt steps braced by retaining logs descend to a footbridge, after which we wind round the hillside, gradually descending to **Fuente Espinel** (Wp.9 60M), where there are stone benches and tiny niches chiselled in the rock to frame twig crosses. Climbing away from the *fuente*, we emerge from the denser woodland into an open area of fern and *brezo*, where we cross in quick succession two dirt tracks (Wp.10 65M) before returning to shady woodland.

This pattern, passing in and out of woodland, is repeated for the next fifty minutes. A few minutes after Wp.10, we re-cross the second dirt track and, twenty-five metres later, at a bend in the dirt track, bear right (SW) on a path descending to a junction (Wp.11 70M). **Fuente Melchora** is ten metres to the right, but we bear sharp left for **El Llanito**, descending to cross a dry watercourse.

Climbing back into the open, we come to a Y-junction next to an electricity pylon, the two branches rejoining some fifty metres later. When the path runs into a dirt track (Wp.12 77M) we maintain direction (SE) for 100 metres, then bear right (W) on another dirt track. The track swings round to the south and climbs gently to another junction (Wp.13 85M) where we take the second branch on the left. The track ends at the **Fuente Aduares** waterpipe (Wp.14 90M) - the *fuente* itself is 75 metres away, shortly after a stone picnic table, and is of no great interest unless you need to fill your water bottle.

Crossing the pipe, we take a path which climbs briefly but steeply to a wayposted junction (Wp.15 93M) where we bear left, descending to join yet another dirt track (Wp.16 95M). Turning left, we descend steadily, passing a small cabin on our left, forty metres metres after which we turn right on a PR signposted path (Wp.17 102M).

This path climbs, which may seem perverse when we're leaving a track that looks all set for a gentle descent to **San Pedro**, but it's worth it, because as the path doubles back (SW) below a large bluff, it passes two extraordinary little shrines, decked out with flowers (synthetic and real) and dozens of plastic icons.

The path continues to a dirt track (Wp.18 115M), where we bear right. When the track joins a tarmac lane (Wp.19 120M), we turn left to cross a bridge and descend to a bend in the **El Pilar** road (Wp.20 130M). Turning left on the alleyway between the road and a grey-and-yellow house, we take a side road descending to another bend in the **El Pilar** road (Wp.21 140M), where we bear left again (NNE) on a concrete lane.

Ignoring a private road branching right, we follow the lane as it bears north and runs into tarmac, descending to the main road between **Breña Alta** and **Mazo**, just south of the bridge over the **Barranco de Aduares** (Wp.22 150M). Rather than following the busy road back to **Breña Alta**, we cross the bridge then, fifty metres later, bear right on the **Camino las Curias**. This pleasant lane leads to the road below the *viveros* in the **Barranco Aguasencio**, where we turn left to climb back to Wp.2. If you feel like a contrast after this peaceful walk, I strongly recommend **Bar Teneguia**, a lively working man's café serving great meatballs, chick-peas, stews and the like.

The **Cumbre Nueva**, the crest linking the volcanoes of **Cumbre Vieja** and the **Caldera de Taburiente**, is one of the classic *mirador* walking routes on La Palma, featuring superbly divergent views over the lush forests on the eastern flank of the spine and the volcanic wasteland above **Llano de Jable**. In this new edition, we explore the crest in two itineraries, the present loop and an interesting linear traverse (Walk 36). The two routes are complementary, so if you have the time, we recommend doing both.

* at the start/finish

Access by bus:
Bus Nº300 runs approximately half-hourly on weekdays and hourly on weekends and fiestas, between **Santa Cruz de la Palma** and **Los Llanos** and stops at opposite the **Visitors' Centre**, or ask the bus driver to stop at the **Centro de Visitantes**. The walk starts from the main car park at the centre.

The car park at the start of the route

Access by car:
The walk starts from the main **El Paso Centro de Visitantes** car park, alongside the **LP-3** road running west-east across the island. The car park is 50 metres west of the entrance to the visitors' centre. There is a second, smaller car park a little further along the main road.

From the main visitors' centre car park (Wp.1 0M), we follow **Calle Calderón** (N) for 250 metres until a dirt-track in front of a solitary tree protected by a stone-wall branches off to the right (Wp.2 4M E) onto the **Camino de la Garza** nature trail (**PR-LP 1.1**). Turning right, we follow the PR, strolling between dry-stone walls and enjoying the bucolic countryside. After passing several *paredones* (pyramid-shaped heaps of stones cleared from the farmland), we reach a tarmac lane (Wp.3 20M NW). Turning left, we follow this lane (NW) for 700 metres until it joins the **PR-LP 1** (Wp.4 33M E). Turning right, we climb steadily to reach the **Ermita Virgen del Pino** (Wp.5. 42M), behind which two dirt tracks climb into the woods.

Ignoring the fainter track to the left and a path branching right, we take the main track for 'Santa Cruz' (**Camino Real de los Puertos**). The track is soon obscured by a dense blanket of pine needles, but ignoring all branches and staying to the right of a long, tumble-down wall, we climb steadily along a wooded spur (NE), till we come to a signposted turn-off to the left, for 'La Cumbrecita via Camino de Gordian' (Wp.6. 53M). Carrying straight on, we continue climbing on a distinct donkey trail, sometimes called the **Camino del Reventón**.

Zigzagging up the donkey trail (signposted 'Santa Cruz') we climb above the woods to barer, rockier terrain where the spur narrows and steepens, and the switchbacks get tighter. The views improve the higher we go, until a long straight stretch brings us to the final couple of switchbacks, and we emerge at the **Reventón** pass on the **Pista Hilera de la Cumbre** (Wp.7 100M), beside a small water tap and in front of a long stone bench overlooking **Santa Cruz**.

Turning right, we follow the **GR-131** along the dirt track (S), all the way to the **El Pilar** road, passing several antennae after half-an-hour. After forty-five minutes, we can see to the west, at the head of a long grey lava flow, two small volcanoes. The higher, broken crater is **Montaña Quemada**, the better formed smaller crater **Montaña de Enrique**. Our return route passes between these two volcanoes. The track gets rather dusty and monotonous toward the end, but fine views of **Birigoyo** (see Walk 7) compensate in the final stretches before the road (Wp.8 180M).

Bearing right, we follow the road down to the **El Pilar Área Recreativa/Zona de Acampada**, where a signpost indicates the 'PR-14 Llanos del Jable / El Paso / Tacande' (Wp.9 183M). Forty metres further down the road, we bear right through a gap in the *zona de acampada* fence, bringing us round to the left of the 'sentry-box' shower cabins, perched over a shallow watercourse. We cross the camping area running parallel to the watercourse until, at the NW corner, ten metres from the end of the fence, the watercourse flattens out and feeds into a yellow-and-white PR-waymarked path.

The path, faint at first, soon becomes clearer as it tunnels through the woods, emerging in a gully alongside a huge bank of *picón* before descending to cross the road (Wp.10 200M). Crunching coarse *picón* underfoot, we descend to a bend in the road, where we bear left (Wp.11 205M) on a broad track across the bleak, exposed slopes behind **Montaña Quemada**. At a wayposted Y-junction (Wp.12 210M), we bear right towards the small wooded **Montaña de Enrique**, and then right again at the next Y-junction (Wp.13 215M).

After a steady descent, we reach a bend in a major dirt track (Wp.14 227M), where we bear right on a broad trail, descending to cross another dirt track (Wp.15 230M) which we rejoin thirty metres lower down. Bearing left, we follow the dirt track and, just after it runs into a tarmac lane, turn right to recover the broad trail (Wp.16 232M). The trail widens to a dirt track, first crossing the lane (Wp.17 240M) then joining it at a junction with a track for **La Montañeta** (Wp.18 245M).

Following the lane down to a Y-junction (Wp.19 255M), we bear left on a dirt track cutting out a loop in the lane. Ignoring a red-waymarked branch to the west, we follow this track (N) until it rejoins the lane (265M), which we stick to all the way to the main road (Wp.20 275M). Bearing right, we follow the main road back to our starting point.

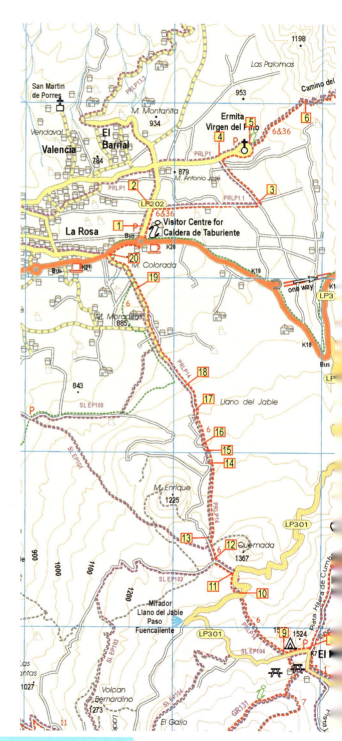

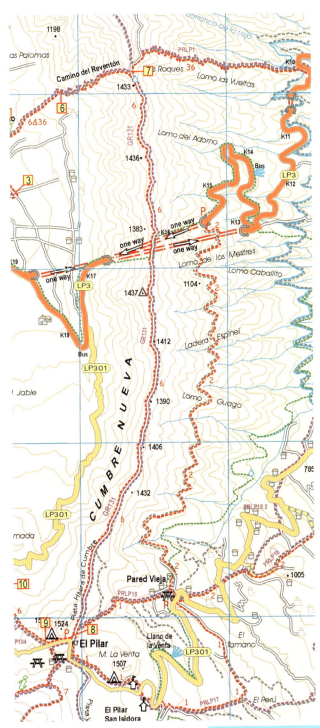

7 CUMBRE VIEJA: PICO BIRIGOYO

Pico Birigoyo is the northernmost of the high volcanic peaks along the **Cumbre Vieja** and an ideal introduction to the famous **Ruta de los Volcanes**. It's a relatively easy walk, but gets a 4 rating for exertion due to the rough paths at the top and the steep descent. Not recommended when there's poor visibility or a strong wind. Walking boots are pretty much essential - anyone wearing sports shoes will end up with a footfull of grit.

Access: by car. Park opposite the **El Pilar Área Recreativa** at km 6.8 of the **LP-301**.

Our start at the recreation area (Wp.1)

From the **El Pilar** parking area (Wp.1 0M), we take the **GR-131** for 'Los Canarios', crossing the *área recreativa* and passing the main administrative block (there are public toilets behind this building), beyond which the **Ruta de los Volcanes** begins (Wp.2 3M).

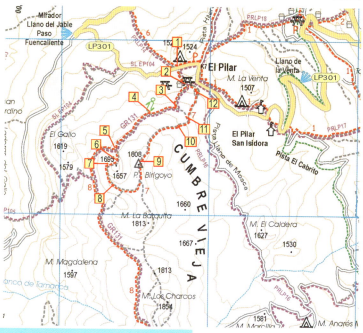

Following a broad path signposted 'Fuencaliente/Los Canarios' through the pine, we climb steadily, zigzagging up to a junction (Wp.3 15M), where we turn sharp right to continue on the **GR-131**.

The path gradually emerges from the tree cover with fine views to the north, passing the **Mirador del Birigoyo** orientation picture board (Wp.4 20M). The pine are more widely scattered as we climb alongside the base of **Birigoyo** and get our first glimpse of *picón*, the grey volcanic grit that covers the **Cumbre Vieja**. Approaching what appears to be a small, discrete cone, we leave the GR and bear left on a path currently marked by a truncated signpost (Wp.5 30M).

This slippery, gritty path climbs steeply, splintering at the top before emerging on a breach in the **Volcán de San Juan** (Wp.6 40M). Turning right, we climb a faint cairn-marked way over rocks studded with pink houseleeks. When the path levels out after a large boulder (Wp.7 50M), we ignore several parallel paths lower down, and stay near the rim. Splendid views of the coast, dominated by the lighthouse of **La Bombilla**, open up down to our right. Passing a small windbreak (Wp.8 55M), we ignore two paths branching to the right and gradually circle the crater till we're heading due north on a broad clear path leading to the **Pico Birigoyo** trig point (Wp.9 70M), from where we have superb views through 360 degrees.

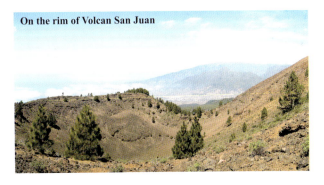
On the rim of Volcan San Juan

To descend, we take the clear path snaking away toward the **Pista Hilera de la Cumbre** (NE), zigzagging at first then skittering through *picón*, skirting a partial crater before recovering the shade of the pine (Wp.10 85M). Our narrow path now winds through and along the edge of the pine forest before switching back to the head of a broad firebreak (Wp.11 90M).

There are several paths descending through the woods beyond the firebreak, but the simplest way down is along the firebreak itself, ignoring tracks branching off onto the flanking terraces, until we reach a stone fire-fighting building (Wp.12). At this point, we leave the firebreak and follow the path to the left (NW) through the heart of the woods to rejoin our outward route at Wp.2.

Of all the walks in La Palma, this is The Big One that walkers feel they have to do - understandably, as nature, with a little help from humankind, has forged a perfect day-hike following the stunning line of volcanoes strung along the **Cumbre Vieja** like so many humps on some fantastical sea monster. The route is strenuous, but not as mammoth as its reputation; expecting to take six hours, I finished in five, breaks included - bear this in mind, I may have had an uncommonly quick day!

The described itinerary follows the **GR-131**, which studiously avoids some of the more spectacular rim sections of the traditional route - variations can be concocted using Walks 7&9, while a more adventurous Over The Top alternative is indicated in the text. A lot of work has been done on the path, until 1920 the main land link between **Fuencaliente** and **Santa Cruz**; though rarely rough underfoot, good boots are still advisable. It's well waymarked and regularly signposted and, as described, poses no problems of vertigo. Wind and mist can be a problem, but even if **El Pilar** is under cloud, the crest maybe clear. It's generally fresh on top, even in summer, but the sun is intense, and the descent to **Fuencaliente** (signposted 'Los Canarios') can be infernal.

Our start at El Pilar

* in **Fuencaliente**. The **Bar/Restaurante Centauria** serves good, fresh tapas and the excellent **Patio del Vino** provides slightly more sophisticated cuisine.

Access by taxi: to **El Pilar**. Return by bus N° 200 or 201 from **Fuencaliente**.

Following Walk 7 to Wp.5 (30M), we ignore the **Birigoyo** path and continue on the **GR-131** (WSW) which descends slightly to join a broad dirt track (Wp.6 40M) and the **SL-104** from **El Paso** (the **SL-105** link with Walk 11 joins the track a little way to the north; both are alternative ways onto the present itinerary). Maintaining a southerly bearing, we climb steadily up the track, ignoring several branch paths on the left and one track to the right.

As the track bears east for **Birigoyo**, we branch right (SE) on a broad trail (Wp.7 55M) signposted 'Los Canarios'. Winding through the pine, we climb very slightly, possibly wondering where all the volcanoes are, the only evidence so far being the debris scattered between the trees. Our first clue comes as the pine become more sparse and a couple of small conical peaks appear to the east. After climbing a small rise, we descend slightly in sight of

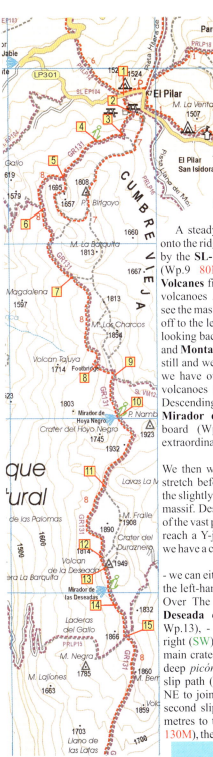

the superbly mottled head of the **Barranco de Tamanca**. A long level stretch skirts **Montaña de los Charcos**, before the path swings sharp left and climbs to cross a footbridge over a gully (Wp.8 75M).

A steady climb (E then S) brings us onto the ridge, where the **GR-131** is joined by the **SL-125** from **Llano de la Mosca** (Wp.9 80M), and the **Ruta de los Volcanes** finally declares its kinship with volcanoes … with a vengeance: first we see the massive block of **Pico Nambroque** off to the left; climbing a little further and looking back north, we see **Pico Birigoyo** and **Montaña de Barquita**; a little further still and we reach a platform, from where we have our first stunning views of the volcanoes stretching away to the south. Descending from here, we reach the **Mirador de Hoyo Negro** information board (Wp.10 85M) overlooking the extraordinary crater of the same name.

We then wind through a lightly wooded stretch before coming back into view of the slightly daunting **Duraznero-Deseada** massif. Descending on a ridge to the west of the vast pitchy **Malforada** lava flow, we reach a Y-junction (Wp.11 105M) where we have a choice:

- we can either carry straight on, following the left-hand branch onto the wilder route Over The Top -in every sense- of the **Deseada** craters (rejoining the GR at Wp.13), - or (as mapped), we can bear right (SW) to follow the GR, skirting the main craters. After a long trudge through deep *picón*, we climb steeply, passing a slip path (Wp.12 125M) branching back NE to join the Over The Top route. At a second slip path, we double back a few metres to the **Deseada** trig point (Wp.13 130M), the highest elevation on the walk.

Looking north from Deseada

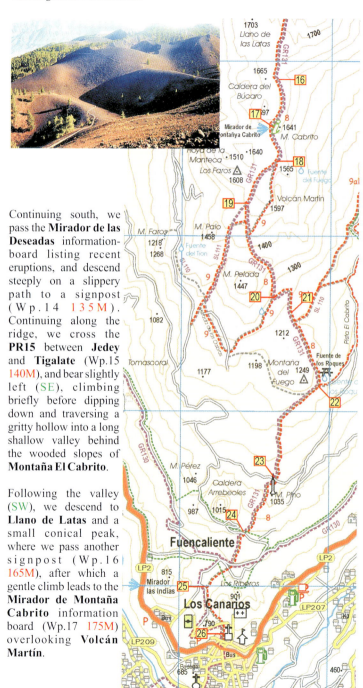

Continuing south, we pass the **Mirador de las Deseadas** information-board listing recent eruptions, and descend steeply on a slippery path to a signpost (Wp.14 135M). Continuing along the ridge, we cross the **PR15** between **Jedey** and **Tigalate** (Wp.15 140M), and bear slightly left (SE), climbing briefly before dipping down and traversing a gritty hollow into a long shallow valley behind the wooded slopes of **Montaña El Cabrito**.

Following the valley (SW), we descend to **Llano de Latas** and a small conical peak, where we pass another signpost (Wp.16 165M), after which a gentle climb leads to the **Mirador de Montaña Cabrito** information board (Wp.17 175M) overlooking **Volcán Martín**.

Volcán Martín

Descending to a Y-junction north of **Volcán Martín** (Wp.18 180M), we bear right (see Walk 9 for the crater branch). Skirting to the west of the volcano, we pass three branch paths down to the **SL-111**, the third of which is signposted (Wp.19 185M).

The GR then descends to the east of **Montaña Pelada**'s twin peaks, passing another signpost, soon after which we veer sharp left (Wp.20 200M) to descend steeply then steadily east. At successive signposts, we bear right to resume our southerly direction then, a couple of minutes later, left (Wp.21 205M), leaving the broad trail and taking a narrower path channelled by low stone walls.

After crossing the **SL-110 Vereda de las Cabras**, we skirt to the east of **Montaña del Fuego**, passing a signposted turning on our left down to 'Fuente Los Roques' (Wp.22 215M) an *área recreativa* with water, picnic tables and barbecues, and in an emergency a forest guard with a walkie-talkie. The GR circles behind **Montaña del Fuego**, descending toward the antenna-topped **Montaña del Pino**. After a long, steady descent through young pine, we cross the dirt track (Wp.23 230M) linking the **Pistas del Oeste** and **Este** (the tracks flanking the **Cumbre Vieja**) and curve to the west of **Montaña del Pino**, crossing another dirt track and bearing left on a broad trail that initially runs parallel to the track.

The trail narrows, descending gently between 'kerb' stones to a rougher, slightly steeper stretch, after which low walls define the clear path we follow nearly all the way to **Fuencaliente**. After crossing the **Fuencaliente** dirt track (Wp.24 240M), the walled path intersects with the **GR-130** and crosses the track again. At the third junction with the track (Wp.25 250M), we bear left and follow the track. Shortly after a branch on the right down to the football field (which doubles as a campsite), we leave the dirt track, bearing left on a signposted path that brings us within sight of **Fuencaliente**.

Crossing the track (now surfaced) for the last time, we descend past the tennis courts to the church (Wp.26 270M) from where we stroll down to the main road for refreshment, transport and accommodation.

Compared to the lush foliage of the north, the south can seem excessively austere, but once you get up in the mountains, what looks bleak from below becomes a fascinating puzzle of delicately shaded rock and deep craters crammed together like a crumpled honeycomb. Using the tail end of the traditional **Ruta de los Volcanes**, the route followed by the **GR-131**, and two *senderos locales*, this circuit provides an excellent introduction to the region. In summer, start early to avoid the midday heat. For shorter versions, see the alternative at the end of the main walk description.

Access by car:
By car on a well-made dirt road, but check first with the Tourist Information Office that the track has not been damaged by storm erosion. From **Fuencaliente**, turn left fifteen metres north of the DISA petrol station (km25.6 of the **LP-2**), setting the odometer at zero, and follow the signs for 'Inst. Deportivas – Campo de Futbol'. Turn right three hundred metres later, then left after another 100 metres. Ignoring branches down to the football field, bear right at the Y-junction at km1.8 (where the tarmac ends), then left at km 2.7, and right at km6.5. The walk starts at km7.

The start at Wp.1

From the junction at km7 (Wp.1 0M), our path climbs steeply then steadily to cross the **SL-110 Vereda de las Cabras** (Wp.2 10M), signposted 'Pista del Este' to the right, 'Fuente del Tión' to the left. We maintain direction (NE) on the **SL-111**, trudging steadily up a long, broad, gritty path behind the western dome of **Montaña Pelada**, gradually bringing **Volcán Martín** into view before emerging on a small rise (Wp.3 40M) within sight of a GR signpost.

The **SL-111** maintains direction (NE) to join the GR at the signpost, but for a gentler climb, we bear right (ENE) and cross a thin fringe of young pine flanking the GR. Turning left on the clearly trodden GR (Wp.4 43M), we pass the official junction with the SL (Wp.5 50M) and climb through *picón* to a broad col (Wp.6 60M). Crossing the col, we ignore a minor path to the left and climb to a waypost (Wp.7 65M), where we leave the GR, turning sharp right onto **Volcán Martín**. At the junction thirty metres later, we bear right, climbing round the rim of the crater to the red, 1597 metre summit at its southern tip (Wp.8 75M).

To descend, we take the boot-churned reddish route to the SW. Using the controlled-skid technique, we skitter down at a hell of a lick (there's no choice about this, but don't build up too much speed as the *picón* is shallower and less skiddable lower down) to rejoin the GR (Wp.9 85M). Breaks aren't normally scheduled, but everyone will have boots full of grit here, so I've allowed a few minutes for pouring out the *picón*.

Bearing left, we follow the **GR-131** for a more sedate descent, skirting to the west of the twin peaks of **Montaña Pelada** and passing a GR signpost (Wp.10 90M). When the GR turns sharp left at a second signpost (Wp.11 95M), we carry straight on for 'Fuente del Tión/Al Vereda de las Cabras' on a clear, rock-lined path winding between pine and passing on our right a small, dry *fuente* (Wp.12 98M). After a gentle descent, gradually curving round to the west, we cross a dirt track (Wp.13 105M) and join the **Vereda de las Cabras.** Continuing in the direction of 'Fuente del Tión/Pista del Oeste' (WNW), we cross the minor track climbing from our starting point (Wp.14 15M) and rejoin our outward route at Wp.2, where we turn left to return to the car.

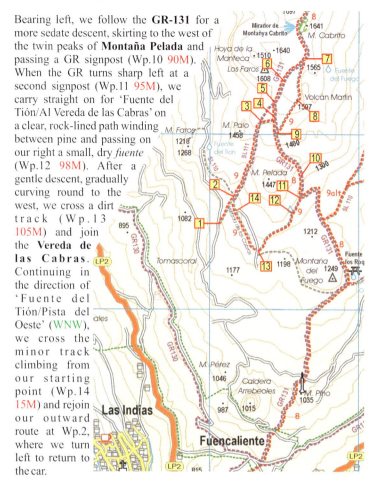

Alternative versions: (Walk 9 alt) Under the Volcano

Not necessarily shorter, but considerably easier, traversing the extraordinary lava-scape below **Volcán Martin**.

2 walker, 55 or 125 minutes (see text),7.5km, 100 metres ascents/descents circuit

Access by car:
Before setting out check with the Tourist Information Office that the dirt road to **Fuente de los Roques** is driveable. Take the 'Fuente de los Roques/Pino de la Virgen' lane at km23.2 of the **LP-2**, setting the odometer at zero. This intersection should be signposted by the time we go to print, but if not, the lane is readily identifiable thanks to a distinct pine surrounded by low walls right in the middle of the junction. The tarmac ends at a sharp-left bend after 1.2 km.

Continuing on dirt track, follow the signs for 'Fuente de los Roques' ignoring all branch tracks.

The alternative versions start from the **Fuente de los Roques Área Recreativa**, 5.2km from the main road.

Turn off from main road to Fuente de los Roques

From inside the *área recreativa* (Wp.1 0M), take the **Monte del Fuego** path up to the **GR-131** (Wp.2 10M). Turn right for **El Pilar** and right again at the junction with the **SL-110 Vereda de las Cabras** (Wp.3 25M). After crossing a moonscape of jagged black lava, the green and white *vereda* swings sharp right (Wp.4 35M) between two large cairns.

Wp.1, from the recreation area

Either turn right to follow the *vereda* down to the **Pista el Cabrito** (Wp.5 40M) or continue straight ahead (NE), on a narrower path marked with smaller cairns that winds through the woods to join the *pista* further on (Wp.6 80M). In either case, return along the **Pista el Cabrito** to the *área recreativa*, fifteen minutes from Wp.5, thirty-five minutes from Wp.6.

San Antonio and Teneguía are La Palma's best known volcanoes, largely thanks to accessibility and the fact that Teneguía erupted in 1971. The paths are perhaps not the most interesting the island has to offer, but they do complement La Palma's wide palette of landscape types, giving us a hint of what walking on Lanzarote is like, and the views are superb. There's a slight risk of vertigo on Teneguía, which can be dangerous when the wind's strong .

Access by car:

The walk starts near or at (depending upon whether you choose to pay the fee to visit and park at **Volcán San Antonio**) the **Volcán San Antonio Visitors' Centre** entrance gate. Alternatively, one could start at **Fuencaliente** (see 'Access by bus' below) or, using the extension, **Faro de Fuencaliente** (bus Nº203).

At the Visitors' Centre

If arriving by car, take the **LP-209** from **Fuencaliente** down towards **Las Indias**. The turn-off to **Volcán San Antonio Visitors' Centre** comes after 1.1 km. There is an entry fee of €5 per person onto **Volcán San Antonio**, which includes parking in the visitors' centre car-park. Alternatively, park on the lane just above the entrance gate.

Access by bus:

Bus Nºs 200, 201, & 203 stop at **Fuencaliente**. From the bus stop in **Fuencaliente**, follow the main street to the west for 200 metres, then take the **GR-131** / cobbled lane down to the left (**Calle Emilio Quintana Sanchez**) between a small supermarket and the **Bar Junonia**. Continue along **Calle los Volcánes**, eventually crossing the **LP-209** and emerging in front of the **Volcán San Antonio Visitors' Centre**.

Our starting point is 50 metres NE of the **Centro de Visitantes** entrance gate (Wp.1 0M). The optional visit to the **Volcán San Antonio** involves a brief detour via the visitors' centre. If you do opt for this, after going through the visitors' centre, we follow the western rim of the crater (not particularly colourful but perfectly formed and very large) to the 632 metre trig point (Wp.2 15M), from where we have great views over **Volcán Teneguía** and the coast. Unfortunately, a full circuit of the crater is no longer permitted, so we retrace our steps (see photo over the page) back to Wp.1, and head east on a tarmac lane. This is the start of the walk for those who skip **Volcán San Antonio.**

The lane brings us almost immediately to a junction with a dirt track in front of

Heading back from Wp.2 to Wp.1

a water tap (Wp.3 32M) where we bear right.

Three hundred and fifty metres later, shortly before the track swings left (E), we bear right on a broad, gritty way (Wp.4 38M) descending toward the upper **Canal de Fuencaliente**, which is capped with concrete and clearly visible.

Crossing the canal, we see **Teneguía** again, and begin the usual controlled-skid descent through *picón*.

After emptying our boots beside the vineyards at the bottom, we descend to a broad track (Wp.5 53M) and turn right, bearing left fifty metres later to descend along a narrower dirt track (Wp.6 54M). The narrower track soon runs along another covered canal to reach a junction (Wp.7 69M). Later on, we will continue to the right, but first we bear left for an exciting climb up **Volcán Teneguía.**

You may think there's no point climbing **Teneguía** having had a superior perspective from **San Antonio**, but it's worth it because the views are even better, including the shattered rim of the crater and the tormented, fractured lava

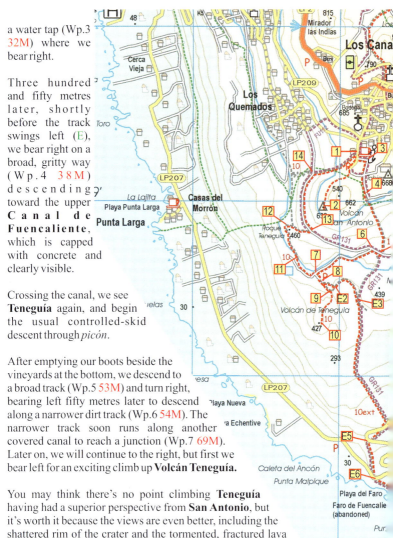

flows to the east. After just over a hundred metres, we ignore a branch to the left (Wp.8 71M) (the **GR-131** descends over a vast lava field to **Faro de Fuencaliente**, see the Extension below) and bear right.

At the Y-junction at the start of the climb (Wp.9 75M), we bear right again.

After crossing a narrow, exposed ridge, we climb steeply and skirt an outcrop of reddish rock, after which a narrow stretch may give vertigo sufferers some qualms.

Beyond this, it's an easy stroll round to the small pyramid of rocks at the 427 metre summit of **Volcán Teneguía** (Wp.10 85M).

After enjoying the stunning views, we retrace our steps to Wp.7 from where we continue in western direction.

When the track climbs above a large reservoir to the lower **Canal de Fuencaliente** (also known as **Canal del Estado**) (Wp.11 105M), we clamber onto the concrete covered canal and, forty metres further west, bear right on a faint path climbing above the canal to join a broad trail (Wp.12 115M) next to the yellow **Roque Teneguía** (not to be confused with the crater of the same name).

A steady climb on a lava-stone-lined path brings us back to the broad track briefly used after Wp.5 (Wp.13 125M) where we join the **GR-131**. Turning left, we follow the track till the GR branches right (Wp.14 135M) on a clear gritty path climbing steeply through vineyards. After a long, dusty trudge, which in its final stage shadows the **Volcán San Antonio Visitors' Centre** fence, we finally emerge on a tarmac lane (Wp.15 150M) sixty metres above our starting point (Wp.1).

Extension: Faro de Fuencaliente and Playa de Echentive

A gentle descent, but a grim ascent in the heat, so only recommended in cool weather or with a bus or taxi back at the end.

2 walker (one-way), 4 if climbing back up again, 45 minutes (one-way), descent (& ascent) 400 metres.

Note: E2 to E7 are map locators, not GPS waypoints.

The extension starts here, from Wp.8

From Wp.8 (0M) of the main walk, we take the clearly waymarked GR.

Skirting to the right of a mini-crater, we descend into the valley to the east of **Teneguía**, soon joining a broad dirt trail (E2 7M).

Bearing right, we follow the sweep of jagged lava down the valley, bearing right (S) again at a cross-roads of paths (E3 10M) on a narrower but clearly defined path channelled through the volcanic debris.

The lava gradually gives way to finer *picón* and we descend steadily through a lunar landscape to the road (E4 25M), where we bear right. Seventy-five metres later, we turn sharp left to recover the path, partially cutting out a long U-bend in the road. We then cross the road twice more, (E5 & 6 30M & 35M) before coming to the end of the GR at a mapboard (E7 40M) just above the lighthouse and fishing hamlet.

If you haven't time, transport or inclination to climb higher, yet want to see the mess a volcano can make, the **PR-14.1** is the path for you, touring the lava flows (*coladas*) from the **San Juan** volcano, which last erupted in 1949, leaving the **Laderas de Gallo** above **San Nicolás** littered with debris. The route is well waymarked and signposted, and relatively short, but not to be undertaken lightly: the climb is steep, the descent very steep, and the path frequently rough.

Access by car:
Park at the small car park between **Bar Americano** and **Bar San Nicolás**, opposite the southbound bus-stop in **San Nicolás**, at km40.4 of the **LP-2**.

Access by bus:
Bus N° 200 stops (southbound) between **Bar Americano** and **Bar San Nicolás**, in **San Nicolás**, at km40.4 of the **LP-2**.

From the car park (Wp.1 0M), we head north along the *carretera general*, bearing right on the **LP-117** for **Tacande** and, 200 metres later, just after the football field, right again on a PR-signposted track (Wp.2 5M) climbing through volcanic debris. The track, which is partially asphalted, climbs

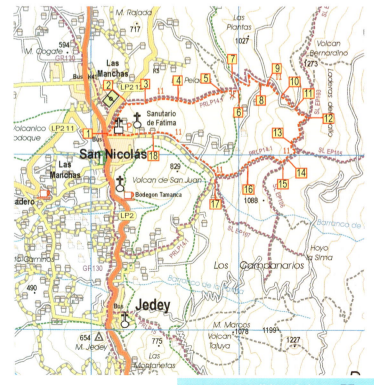

through a bleak, black landscape relieved only by a small terraced vineyard, after the entrance of which (Wp.3 10M), it dwindles to a steep donkey trail that we follow for the next half-hour.

At first the trail is partially paved, but the man-made paving soon gives way to a carpet of lava. Crossing a rough dirt track (Wp.4 20M), we continue climbing steeply past abandoned terraces and scattered pine. The gradient then eases from steep to steady and we cross a narrow, overgrown path (Wp.5 40M), after which we climb gently on a narrower path, maintaining an easterly direction. The lava-paving becomes more slab-like and grainy, then gradually gives way to gritty dirt.

Joining a rough *picón* and cinder dirt track (chained off to our right), we maintain direction to join another better stabilised track (Wp.6 45M), where we turn left, heading north briefly before turning sharp right on another, broader track (Wp.7 50M). This track climbs gently through an infinitely lazy zigzag before coming to a Y-junction (Wp.8 60M), where we take the roughly paved section to the left. The track then widens and swings north, at which point we bear right on a minor track (Wp.9 65M), passing low cliffs of yellow substrata covered by black rock studded with houseleeks. As the track swings left, we bear right to climb a narrow volcanic channel, cutting out a bend before crossing the same track a few metres later (Wp.10 70M). If you catch a whiff of sulphur round here, don't be alarmed: its source is agricultural rather than satanic or volcanic.

Climbing steeply again, we snake our way up a rocky gully (ESE) on a path that is obscure at first but gradually becomes clearer. Re-crossing the dirt track (Wp.11 80M), we climb steadily to the top of the gully and a signposted junction with the **SL-103** to 'El Pilar' and 'El Paso' (Wp.12 90M), where we bear right, sticking to the **PR-14.1** as it meanders through blackened pine to an immense field of lava.

Following the signposted path (and it is a path, though lord knows how they made it) we crunch across pumice stones fragilely colonised by lichen and the odd resolute shrub. Passing a signpost for 'Llano de Tamanca', we traverse a flow of lava that looks like it's still molten (Wp.13 100M) and cross a gully, after which we come to a junction with the **SL-105** to the 'Pista Forestal Principal' (also known as the Pista del Oeste), an alternative way up to the **Ruta de los Volcanes** (see Walk 8). We bear right here, still on the PR, to leave the lava flow and return to a woodland path (Wp.14 105M).

The lava field path (Wps. 12-13)

The path soon joins a minor forestry track, where we bear right, striding along on a bed of pine needles that are pleasantly spongy after the sharp volcanic rock. Enjoy them while you can, because they soon become a liability! At the next junction (Wp.15 110M), the track continues (SW) as the **SL-106** to

'Llano de los Roques', but we bear right for **Llano de Tamanca**, following a broad way, marked with bright blue waymarks as well as the yellow-and-white we've been following so far.

The broad way is obscured by pine needles, but descending (NNW) we soon come to a narrow, clearer path. Unfortunately, it's also very, very steep and carpeted by slippery pine needles that make the descent somewhat precarious.

Carefully, very carefully, picking our way down this path (it's not dangerous, but dignity must be maintained!), we cross an ancient terracing wall (Wp.16 125M), after which the gradient is slightly less aggressive.

Surfaced with loose dirt and *picón*, the path winds down (unfortunately winding so much the controlled-skid method is nearly all control and very little skid) through mixed pine, almond and wild vine. After passing a small stand of chestnut, we emerge into an open area of scrub and prickly pear, where the path becomes firmer underfoot.

Bottom of the steep descent after Wp.16

We then squeeze through an overgrown stretch and pass under a palm tree for the final descent between terraces of vines to a dirt track (Wp.17 145M), just above a narrow tarmac lane that was visible through much of the steep descent.

Leaving the **PR-14.1**, we bear right on the **SL-107**, strolling along the lane (NNW) for a couple of minutes till it swings right and we bear left on a roughly paved track. We stick to this track, maintaining direction when a wider branch swings left to a new house, until we pass two water tanks and join a tarmac lane (Wp.18 160M), which we follow back to our starting point. The bars in **San Nicolás** are good for a drink, but for a real eating experience, head south for 700 metres on the *carretera general* to the troglodytic restaurant, **Bodegón Tamanca**: a bit of a factory, but the food is very good and the setting extraordinary.

A very short walk that earns its itinerary number for the cliff path down to **Puerto Tazacorte**, a modern, pleasantly laid-back resort that has been developed with a degree of discretion (low-rise, multi-coloured, not entirely uniform blocks of flats). It's also the only walk in the book that ends, subject to the usual reservations, with a swim. The route (which is part of the **GR-131**) is reasonably well signposted. There's a slight risk of vertigo.

3 | 2H | 7 km | 600m one way / 600m | 1 | 4

Access: The walk starts at the **Mirador del Time** on the **LP-1** west of **Los Llanos de Aridane**. The *mirador* can be reached by bus Nº100, which links the northern towns. **Puerto Tazacorte** can also be reached from **Los Llanos** by bus Nº207. If arriving by car, we park in the *mirador* car park. If arriving by the Nº207

Our start at Wp.1

or if you're leaving your car in **Puerto Tazacorte**, bus 100 leaves from **Avenida Del Emigrante** on the seafront.

We start immediately north of the *mirador* bar and souvenir shop, on a rough lane (Wp.1 0M) that descends steeply, swinging round to the west of the *mirador*,

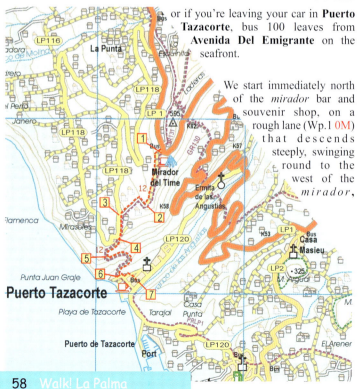

passing several branch tracks into cactus and tabaiba groves.

After a steady to steep descent with fine views along the coast towards **Puerto Naos** and inland towards **Cumbre Nueva**, the lane passes between the perforated walls of a banana plantation, and becomes a dirt track (Wp.2 10M). Turning right a few metres later, we follow a rough track for 100 metres to a triple junction. Turning left twice, first on a track then on another tarmac lane, we descend between hothouses and banana plantations. This stretch of the walk is not a visual treat, but don't despair, the best is yet to come!

At a T-junction backed by a water tank (Wp.3 17M), we turn left (S), passing the beautiful garden of house Nº23. After more gorgeous gardens on both sides of the wide lane, we turn left to descend steeply on a broad signposted path (Wp.4 20M) that's concreted for the first few metres before running into degraded boulder paving.

After a brief but steady descent between an orchard and a banana plantation, we cross the end of a tarmac road in front of a Unipalma warehouse with a corrugated iron roof and a blue door. Near a tall pylon on the opposite side, we recover the roughly paved path, now an authentic donkey trail, bringing us into view of **Tazacorte** beach, which looks completely inaccessible. However, the trail soon passes another great lookout point, the **Mirador del Acantilado del Time**, after which it doubles back (SE) and begins its dramatic descent down the cliff face to **Puerto Tazacorte**.

Views on the descent

Switching back and forth, we descend rapidly, reaching a 100 metre stretch of dirt (Wp.5 30M) interspersed with patches of paving. After a second, longish, easterly stretch on dirt, the paved and dirt sections alternate. We then pass several small caves, many of which are nicely decorated, and some of which were actually inhabited until recently.

Shortly after passing a banana plantation, we emerge on the esplanade between the **Kiosco Teneguía** (Wp.6 45M) and, the only old building in the port, the yellow-painted **Restaurante Taberna del Puerto**. One hundred metres along the promenade, we turn left into **Paseo de los Beatos Martires de Tazacorte** and circle behind the modernist sunken plaza. After passing two fine Indian laurel trees, we bear right to reach the bus-stop (Wp.7 50M).

After enjoying the laid back atmosphere of **Puerto Tazacorte**, energetic souls returning to pick up their car at the **Mirador del Time** may wish to reverse the route. But after enjoying the laid back atmosphere, most people will probably choose to hop on the bus (Nº100)!

This attractive stretch of the **GR-130** is a good introduction to the domestic landscape and ravines of the north-west. Happily, it's littered with signposts, since it criss-crosses a tangle of tarmac lanes, concrete and dirt tracks, paved trails, cobbled and dirt paths, it reads like a complicated wiring diagram. In view of this, I suggest familiarising yourself with the text beforehand, then follow the waymarking on the ground, only referring to the book when in difficulty. Traditionally the itinerary ends at **Tijarafe**, but I've extended it to include the spectacular **Barranco del Jorado** (also spelled **Jurado**), a protected area and nesting ground for rooks, kestrels and rock-doves.

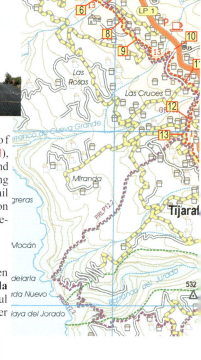

Access by bus:
Bus Nº100 runs between **Santa Cruz de la Palma - Los Llanos**. The walk starts at km80.7 of the **LP-1**.

Bar/Restaurante Tinizara - our start point

From the bus-stop in front of **Bar/Restaurante Tinizara** (Wp.1 0M), we follow the road north for 50 metres and then turn left on a tarmac lane. Descending past a chapel and the **Vino Tendal** retail outlet, we branch right after house N°20 on a partially cobbled trail (Wp.2 9M), re-crossing the lane fifty metres later.

We now descend steadily (WSW) then steeply into the **Barranco de la Baranda** (literally 'handrail', which may be wishful thinking as there's nothing very banister like about it).

The cobbled trail at Wp.2

Crossing the bed of the ravine (Wp.3 20M), our trail climbs to pass a small *mirador* with benches, after which it levels off briefly before descending to cross another lane (Wp.4 25M).

The trail dwindles to an intermittently paved path, winding between abandoned terraces dotted with pine, lichen frosted almond, and prickly pear, before descending to rejoin the lane (Wp.5 30M). Turning left, we follow the lane for fifty metres then bear right on a dirt path supported by a retaining wall, crossing a shallow gully before rejoining the lane.

Shortly after the first house on the left, we branch left on another shortcut path, passing house N°9B before rejoining the lane yet again. When the tarmac turns to concrete, we branch right (Wp.6 40M), recovering the paved trail as it traverses another of the numerous nameless *barrancos* along this coast.

A brief climb brings us onto another tarmac lane, where we bear right. The lane soon runs into a dirt track (Wp.7 45M), from where we get our first glimpse of **Tijarafe**. When the dirt track swings left on a concreted stretch climbing to a tarmac lane, we bear right (Wp.8 50M), recovering the paved trail.

Passing a small avocado plantation, we join a tarmac driveway, which leads us back (yet again!) to the tarmac lane. Bearing right, we follow the lane till it passes a large green house, immediately after which, we bear left (Wp.9 55M) on a dirt path running below the balcony of house N°13.

The path passes several houses, then swings round to cross the **Barranco Pinillo**, after which we climb briefly to join a partially concreted track (Wp.10 65M) below a large, semi-troglodytic dwelling. Bearing right, we follow the track, ignoring all branch paths and tracks, until we pass several new houses built in traditional style and join another tarmac lane (Wp.11 70M).

Turning left, we follow the lane to house N°6 where we take the signposted dirt track to the right. This broad track descends below terraces into the **Barranco de Cueva Grande**, though the *cueva* isn't that *grande*, so you may prefer to call it by its other name, **Barranco Caldereta**, which can be translated as 'little cauldron' or 'lamb stew'! Bearing right below the *cueva*, we leave the track and take a dirt path, which leads to yet another tarmac lane (Wp.12 80M). Crossing the lane, we briefly recover the paved trail before it disappears in tarmac again! Turning left, we climb along the tarmac lane for a little over 100 metres then, opposite a branch lane on the right (the **PR-12.2**), turn left (Wp.13 85M) on a cobbled path climbing to a paved track. Turning right, we soon (inevitably!) rejoin the tarmac lane, which we follow into the outskirts of **Tijarafe**'s modern residential area.

Maintaining direction (SE) past the playground, minimarket and **Casa de la Cultura**, we reach the main road, where we turn right and cross to the 'fishing-smack' car-park. Taking the first turning on the left, signposted 'Bar La Fuente' (Wp.14 95M), we climb towards the church in **Tijarafe**'s old quarter, where we can either carry straight on into **Tijarafe** to wait for the bus in one of the town's bars, or turn left on **Calle El Lomo** to complete the walk.

Ignoring the **Camino El Lomo**, we take the first branch road on the right, leaving the built up area. In front of the green gates of house N°3 and three memorial benches, we bear left on a signposted path (Wp.15 105M). Ignoring a branch to the left, we cross the main road (Wp.16 110M) onto a paved trail into the bed of the **Barranco del Jorado**, where the ravine is divided by a long blade of rock (Wp.17 115M). Descending along the northernmost watercourse, we cross a dull gold water pipe (Wp.18 118M) and turn left up the southernmost watercourse. Thirty metres later, we branch right on a broad dirt path that climbs under a distressingly friable overhang before crossing a pass with superb views up and down the ravine (Wp.19 122M)

After a steady climb, we emerge on the rim of the *barranco* (Wp.20 130M), where we turn left 'al Sendero Local 71' and climb past the **El Jesús** chapel to the main road (Wp.21 135M). The bus-stop is two hundred metres to the south.

El Jesús chapel

Loosely translated this means 'Cliffs of the Little Tiny Walls', suggesting a strong sense of irony in early Hispanic settlers. Following the **SL-TJ71**, we climb from the scattered hamlet of **El Pinar** to the south-western tip of the **Caldera de Taburiente**, and what we get is not 'little tiny walls', but plummeting crags and a birds-eye view of the **Barranco de las Angustias**. Descending via the **GR131** to the **Torre de Time** firewatch tower, we return **to El Pinar** via the **PR-LP10**, also known as 'La Travicsa'.

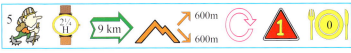

Access by car:
200 metres south of the **El Jesús** turn-off (the **LP-116**), at the 88km marker of the **LP-1** (signposted 'El Pinar'), take the **Camino del Pinar** lane climbing east. Ignore all

The El Pinar plaza near Wp.1

The parking area and Wp.1

branches (including a green sign indicating 'El Pinar' to the right, a much steeper and narrower option) and park 100 metres south-west of the **El Pinar** plaza, in a layby alongside a wall.

Access by bus:
Either climb from **El Jesús** (accessible on the Nº100 bus) on the **SL-TJ71** (+400 metres), or taxi up to **El Pinar** and, at Wp.13, stay on the **GR-131** down to the **Mirador del Time** bar and Walk 12.

From the parking area (Wp.1 0M), we walk 130 metres south and take the green waymarked **SL-TJ71** to the left (Wp.2 2M), climbing steeply on a broad concrete trail between dry-stone walls. After a short, energetic climb, in the course of which we pass two white cupolas of an observatory, we cross a tarmac lane (Wp.3 10M) to join a broad, rocky trail, signposted as the way up to the **Risco las Pareditas** and the **GR131**.

Climbing steeply, as we do throughout the ascent, we cross the concrete track four more times, bearing slightly left after the fifth time, away from a short stretch of abandoned forestry track, after which we cross the dirt track (Wp. 4 20M) linking **Torre del Time** with the **Refugio Tinizara**, and continue on a route marked by a waypost.

The rest of the ascent, on a broad trail/firebreak, is relatively featureless. There are no branches, but nor is there any variety of landscape as we labour

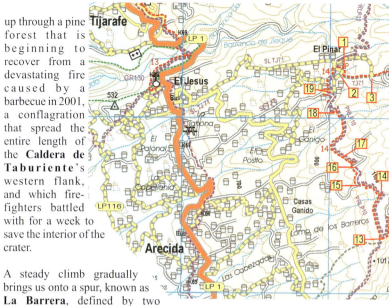

up through a pine forest that is beginning to recover from a devastating fire caused by a barbecue in 2001, a conflagration that spread the entire length of the **Caldera de Taburiente**'s western flank, and which fire-fighters battled with for a week to save the interior of the crater.

A steady climb gradually brings us onto a spur, known as **La Barrera**, defined by two watercourses that ultimately feed into the **Barranco del Jurado**. As the spur narrows so does the trail, dwindling to a path lined with tall thin stones and passing a large charred log in a small pit (Wp.5 50M), after which the path switches back and forth between the northern and southern flanks of the spur, before finally joining the **GR-131** (Wp.6 65M). Our onward route bears right for 'Torre del Time/Puerto de Tazacorte', but first, we turn left and climb a few metres to a superb natural *mirador* overlooking the **Barranco de las Angustias**.

Returning to the **GR-131**, we descend steadily through blackened pine and the cistus that always spring up after a fire, remaining prudently behind the rim of the crater, until we emerge in the deep hollow known as **Hoya Grande** (Wp.7 80M), overlooking **Llanos de Aridane** and the track into the **Barranco de las Angustias**. After a long level stretch, the path descends between terraces of vines, the retaining walls studded with enormous house-leeks, then joins the end of a rough dirt track. Immediately after the first bend we bear left (Wp.8 85M) onto a narrow terrace path which descends briefly, then levels out and joins another dirt track (Wp.9 90M).

Torre del Time firewatch tower

We follow this track, passing branches to the left, right, and left. Fifteen metres after the second left branch, we bear right (Wp.10 95M) on a broad path descending toward the **Torre del Time** firewatch tower, which becomes visible after a minute or so.

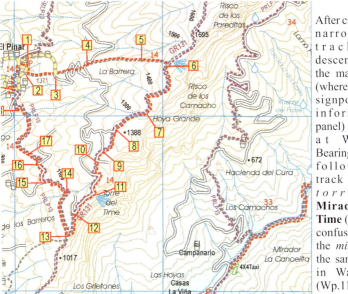

After crossing a narrow dirt track, we descend onto the main track (where there's a signpost and information panel) crossed at Wp.4. Bearing left, we follow this track to the *torre* and **Mirador del Time** (not to be confused with the *mirador* of the same name in Walk 12) (Wp.11 105M).

When the narrow track descending behind the tower swings sharp right, we maintain direction (SW) on a broad rocky trail (Wp.12 110M) down to the signposted junction with the **PR-LP 10** (Wp.13 115M), where we leave the **GR-131** (unless descending to join Walk 12) and turn right onto a narrow path between abandoned terraces. The path dips up and down before winding round to cross a first, unnamed *barranco* choked with ferns (Wp.14 125M).

We then pass a very slightly vertiginous stretch before joining the end of a narrow dirt track, which we follow down to a broader dirt track (Wp.15 130M), where we bear right to maintain our northerly direction. After a gentle climb, the track swings sharp right into a second unnamed *barranco* and we turn left to descend on a waymarked path (Wp.16 135M). The path winds down the flank of the *barranco* before bearing sharp right (E) to cross it, after which a slightly rougher and again, occasionally and very slightly, vertiginous path continues descending (WNW), passing below a large cool cave (Wp.17 140M).

A brief, gentle climb brings us over a small rise, within sight of **El Pinar**, into the triple clefted **Barranco de los Gomeros**. After crossing the three watercourses of the *barranco*, we climb in a westerly direction then, five metres before a cactus backed by a cluster of small pines on the right (Wp.18 153M), double back sharp right and climb steeply to a stone cabin, behind which there's a small reservoir and a line of shady medlar trees.

Just above the reservoir, we bear left on a narrow dirt track, crossing another mini-*barranco* before climbing gently to pass an immense cactus field and join the lane through **El Pinar** (Wp.19 160M). Thirty metres up the lane, we bear left on a cobbled path passing between a cottage and outbuildings. After 150 metres, we turn right to rejoin the lane, on which we turn left to return to the start.

15 CUEVAS DE BURACAS

The **Buracas** caves below **Las Tricias** are popular with guided walking groups, so you need to get there early if you don't want to be queuing up or crowded off the path. Nowadays, most of the deeper caves have become cosy hideaways for the lucky few, but the paths are still attractive, and the Dragon Trees are among the finest on the island.

4 | 2H | 4.5 km | 250m / 250m | 3*

* at Las Tricias Bar/Spar

Access:
By car or bus N°100. Park beside the **Las Tricias Bar/Spar**.

Wp.1, the *ayuntamiento* and Las Tricias

In front of **Las Tricias Bar/Spar**, we take a concrete track descending behind the tiny *ayuntamiento* and playground (Wp.1 0M), where we turn left on a cobbled slip path. Following a very narrow dirt path, we skirt a small orchard, at the end of which,

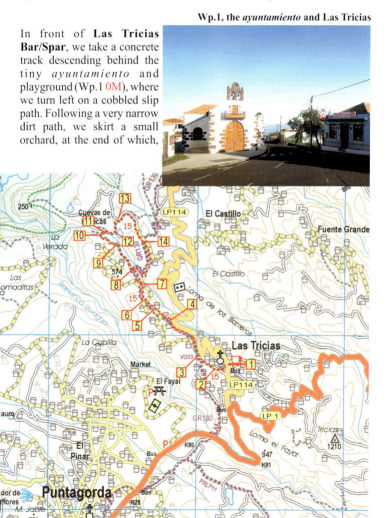

we turn right on a concrete lane that ends after fifteen metres at a small house with ceramic name tiles 'AP' (Wp.2 5M).

We continue descending on a narrow path meandering between gardens, small houses, and abandoned fields, until we come to a T-junction with a broad cobbled alley (Wp.3 10M), where we join the **GR-130**. Turning right, we follow the alley down to the road, where we turn left, descending past **El Café** and a dental clinic to pass between a bottleneck of old houses, fifty metres after which the road swings right and the GR bears left on a broad cobbled track (Wp.4 20M). We leave both the road and, briefly, the GR, taking the cobbled path between the large white building and the house with a triangle painted on its chimney.

The path broadens to a dirt track leading to a tarmac lane, which we descend, rejoining the GR just above a house where you'll probably be charmingly strong-armed into buying some costly almonds, or even a walking stick if you haven't got your wits about you. Immediately after the house (Wp.5 25M), we turn right on a narrow path that rejoins the lane lower down. Just after the next right-hand bend in the lane (Wp.6 30M), we turn left on an access track then immediately right to recover the old path.

The first Dragon Tree

The path descends through an abandoned almond grove, passing the first and largest of the Dragon Trees seen on this itinerary, after which we cross the lane again (Wp.7 35M). Crossing a dirt track a couple of minutes later, we descend past more superb dragon trees to a junction of paths (Wp.8 40M). The GR, which we return on, bears right for **Santo Domingo**, but we continue on the main path, passing a cabin (Wp.9 45M) with a supply line strung across the **Barranco del Corchete**. The path eventually swings right beside a panel advertising orange juice (Wp.10 48M), bringing us into the *barranco*, where we turn right at a T-junction (Wp.11 50M) next to a tiny troglodytic dwelling.

Crossing the *barranco*, we pass the dry **Fuente de Buracas** (Wp.12 53M). Scrambling up natural rock steps, we follow the GR waymarks, crossing the roof of a cave with an immaculately maintained terrace. After traversing a grove of oranges, lemons, grapes and bananas, we emerge on a dirt track beside a GR waypost (Wp.13 60M), where the trudge back up to **Las Tricias** begins.

Turning right, we start climbing, ignoring a first GR branch to the left and continuing on the track as it runs into tarmac. A steady climb brings us to a second wayposted branch for the GR to 'Santo Domingo' (Wp.14 70M), fifteen metres beyond which, we turn right on a dirt track that ends in a small turning circle behind a house. From the turning circle, we continue on a narrow path, re-crossing the **Barranco del Corchete** higher up below a modern aqueduct to rejoin our outward route at Wp.8 (85M).

A short itinerary giving an insight into La Palman rural life and introducing the great **Garafía** pine forest. Using the **PR-LP10**, we traverse the heartland of the local livestock industry, passing rough pasture dotted with skeletal broom picked bare by goats, and land stripped of *brezo* and laurel for summer feed when the goats are shut away. We then climb through the fringes of the **Pinar de Garafía Nature Reserve** before descending back through farmland to **El Bailadero** restaurant.

Restaurante El Bailadero & parking 50m south of Wp.1

Access:
By car or bus N°100. Park in the lay-by above **El Bailadero** at km63.8 of the **LP-1**, a little way north of the junction with the **Roque de los Muchachos** road.

We start just below the restaurant on a narrow dirt track (E) for 'La Mata' (Wp.1 0M) - the **PR-LP10** whose route we follow to waypoint 5. The track soon dwindles to a drovers' trail, dropping into the **Barranco de los Sables**, where it joins another, broader dirt track (Wp.2 5M).

The signposted dirt track at the start (Wp.1)

Bearing right, we curve behind the bare **Montaña Vaqueros**, passing a major branch to the right (Wp.3 8M), which is our return route.

Maintaining our easterly direction, we ignore all branches and stick to the main track which eventually becomes a tarmac lane (Wp.4 20M). Again ignoring all branches, we follow the lane as it winds through the countryside before climbing to the fringes of the **Garafía** forest, passing a stand of immensely tall pine.

When the lane joins the main road (Wp.5 35M), we turn right, leaving the PR. After 100 metres, just before the next bend in the road, we bear right on a dirt track climbing past a small farm. Climbing steadily through deep, peaceful woods, we pass a water-hut, just after which we branch left at a Y-junction (Wp.6 45M).

Maintaining our southerly direction and still climbing steadily, we ignore all branches until the track bears right (SW) bringing us to a second Y-junction (Wp.7 55M) where we fork right and right again at a third Y-junction a couple of minutes later.

Our track now winds round the mountainside, with fine views over the farmland round **Montaña Vaqueros**. Immediately after passing a branch to the south, we bear left at a Y-junction (Wp.8 60M). We now cross two shallow *barrancos*, the first topped by terraces of vines, the second choked with fern, before climbing to join a track (Wp.9 70M) leading to a house thirty metres above the junction.

Maintaining our westerly direction, we follow a grey water pipe above terraced pasture till we reach a T-junction (Wp.10 75M), where we turn right and start descending. Reaching a second T-junction just above a large circular reservoir (Wp.11 80M), we turn left to pass above apple orchards, then bear right on another track a couple of minutes later, rejoining our outward route at Wp.3 (90M).

If Robert Mitchum were a town, he'd be **Santo Domingo de Garafía**. It's sleepy, a bit dead and alive, and doesn't seem to be doing very much most of the time, but it does have an undeniable presence and a nonchalant, somnolent charm all of its own. The sort of place to linger and drink up the atmosphere, providing the atmosphere isn't battering you over the head with breathtaking gusts of wind, which it often is. A mix of tidy domesticated landscape and untamed elemental wilderness, our itinerary follows the **PR-9** and **GR-130** on bucolic lanes, cobbled donkey trails and sinuous dirt tracks.

| 3 | 2H | 10 km | | 200m / 700m | one way | 4 |

Wp.1, the bus station

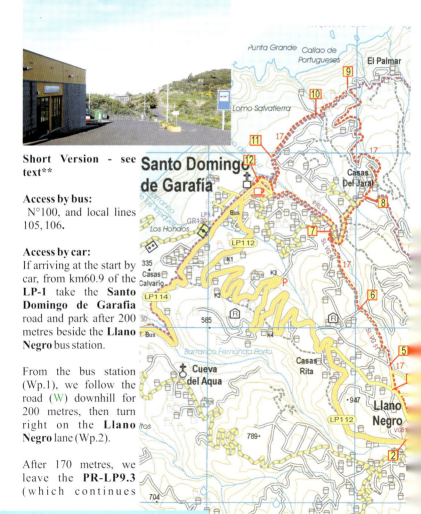

Short Version - see text**

Access by bus:
N°100, and local lines 105, 106.

Access by car:
If arriving at the start by car, from km60.9 of the **LP-1** take the **Santo Domingo de Garafia** road and park after 200 metres beside the **Llano Negro** bus station.

From the bus station (Wp.1), we follow the road (W) downhill for 200 metres, then turn right on the **Llano Negro** lane (Wp.2).

After 170 metres, we leave the **PR-LP9.3** (which continues

Wp.2 Llano Negro turnoff

straight on along a cobbled lane to **San Antonio del Monte** and **Palmar**) and turn left on a tarmac lane descending between houses (Wp.3).

Maintaining a northerly direction, we descend steeply into open countryside, where we take the second track on the right, next to a doorway, the lone relic of a ruin (Wp.4 8M).

Signpost at Wp.3

Strolling along the partially cobbled track, we bear right at a Y-junction, after which the track briefly dwindles to a trail.

The doorway at 8 minutes

Ignoring two branches on the left leading to small houses, we continue on the track as the semi-agricultural heath land of **Llano Negro** gradually gives way to young pine forest, where we bear right at a second Y-junction. After crossing a dirt track (Wp.5 20M), we continue descending on a narrow donkey trail through mixed heath land and wind-chafed pine.

The trail runs alongside the **Barranco de la Luz**, gradually broadening into an ancient paved cart track. A steep descent, some of it badly eroded, brings us within sight of **Santo Domingo**. Crossing the tip of a concrete track (Wp.6 35M), we continue on the donkey trail before rejoining the track, which we follow for 200 metres. Shortly after passing a car-port, on our right, and a path to our left, we reach a branch path (Wp.7 40M) doubling back on the right (SE) toward a tarmac lane, behind which there's a large water pipe.

For the short walk (15M to **Santo Domingo), we stay on the concrete track, which soon runs into an immaculately cobbled section of the lane, the official, signposted junction with the 'PR9'. From here, we simply follow the cobbled cart track alongside the **Barranco de la Luz** into the outskirts of **Santo Domingo**, where we bear right on a tarmac lane down to the green 'tower' block of the main walk (see below).

For the main walk, we turn right at Wp.7. The path descends to a dirt track, which leads onto the tarmac lane and the **PR-9**. We follow the PR along the lane (NE), passing an asphalted branch descending north-west, shortly after which our lane runs into a dirt track (Wp.8 50M) and we leave the PR, turning left on a concrete track signposted 'Casa Turismo Rural Isla Bonita'.

When the concrete ends, we ignore the 'Casa Rural' branch to the left and continue (NE) on the dirt track through a series of long switchbacks as it repeatedly approaches then shies away from the nameless *barranco* that descends from the **Casas del Jaral** to the west of the tiny hamlet of El Palmar. After a final approach to the *barranco*, at the bottom of which we can see dragon trees and cactus spurge nestling in the folds of the ravine, the track passes a **GR-130** signpost (Wp.9 80M) and we turn left for **Santo Domingo** on a broad path alongside a wire mesh fence.

The path, in fact another donkey trail, climbs gently (SW) before crossing a rough dirt track (Wp.10 90M). After a steadier climb, the brightly painted houses of **Santo Domingo** come into view and we first cross then join another track, dirt when we cross it, concrete when we join it, at the end of which (Wp.11 100M), barely a stone's throw from **Santo Domingo**, we are confronted by the dramatic gulf of **Barranco de la Luz**. The concrete ends behind a small house on the edge of the ravine, and we continue on the old paved way, a beautiful trail snaking through the crooked 'M' of the ravine, the walls of which are dotted with caves housing dozens of goats, the cliffs sheltering more dragon trees and spurge.

A final steep climb brings us into **Santo Domingo** behind a tall green building, the town's token 'tower' block, beyond which we emerge in the main square beside the pleasant **Bar/Cafeteria Plaza** (Wp.12 110M). The bus stop is 200 metres further west, just past the **Bar/Restaurant Taberna Santy**. There are two restaurants in town, neither of them open when we visited. Two hundred metres west of the bus stop is the **El Bernegal Restaurant**, which is more upmarket than our usual *tipicos*.

There's a touch of the Grand-Old-Duke-of-Yorks about this one: we march down the hill, then we march up the hill, then we turn round and do it all over again! Logical, it ain't, but logic goes out the window on La Palma's northern coast, where walks that are 'logical' in terms of coherence are bonkers when you calculate the accumulated climb.

We start from the village of **El Tablado**, sandwiched between the **Barrancos de Fagundo** and **de los Hombres**, the two biggest ravines in the **Guelguén Nature Reserve**. Despite mass migration (the population is a tenth of what it once was), the village has clung onto existence just as it clings onto its precarious perch between the ravines, and even boasts an excellent restaurant, **El Moral**. Our route crosses the **Fagundo** on the old coastal path, now part of the **GR-130**, linking **El Tablado** with the hamlet of **Don Pedro**, a pleasant enough place, but not really worth the extra 20 minutes and 100 metres once we've crossed the ravine. The pleasure is all in exploring the monumental and otherwise inaccessible **Fagundo**, with its magnificent cliffs, caves to gladden a hermit's heart, and a glut of weird and wonderful cacti.

Don't be deceived by the insignificant little squiggle representing this itinerary on the map. As the crow flies, it's barely a kilometre long, but walkers aren't crows and this is a strenuous walk. There's a slight risk of vertigo on the western flank of the ravine, otherwise the main hazard is for arachnophobes, the path being criss-crossed by dozens of spiders webs.

5 | 2¾ H | 6.5 km | 700m / 700m | out & back | 1 | 5

Access by car:
The **Tablado** turn-off from the main **LP-1** road is at km55.1 The walk starts in the middle of **El Tablado**. Simply follow the concrete lane until you see the 'GR/PR' signpost. There's one parking space beside an abandoned house just below the start. That said, the concrete lane is very narrow and very steep. If your car is big, cumbersome or unfamiliar, you may prefer to park towards the end of the tarmac near the **El Moral** restaurant.

Note: GPS reception is erratic over most of the route and the gps waypoints should be regarded as 'map location' markers rather than navigation points.

Our start at Wp.1

From the village centre (Wp.1 0M), we take the **GR-130** for **Santo Domingo**, a broad path with mock petroglyphs and cave-paintings etched into patches of concrete.

After circling to the west of abandoned terraces and passing a couple of dragon trees, we join a paved path heading towards the sea, leaving behind the last house in the village, and descending onto a narrow spur overlooking the *barranco*.

The paved way declines to a rocky path and we enter the **Reserva Natural de Guelguén** (Wp.2 15M). After zigzagging down with great views along the coast beyond **La Fajana**, **El Tablado**'s landing when contact with the outside world was by boat, we swing round the spur and enter the *barranco* below patchwork cliffs undermined by shallow caves. Taking care not to slip on the unstable gravel, we descend steeply, passing a tremendous variety of spurge and houseleeks, and one or two deeper caves, before finally reaching the bottom of the *barranco* (Wp.3 30M).

I don't really need to tell you what comes next, as you'll have been looking at it all the way down. Starting our ascent, we pass what must have been an impressive waterfall, and climb round a very slightly vertiginous ledge. The path then levels out above abandoned terraces and below a long, snout-like spur (Wp.4 40M). Winding up the spur, we swing right on another slightly vertiginous stretch, after which a final zigzagging climb out of the *barranco* brings us to a Y-junction (Wp.5 65M).

Bearing left on the broader, rockier path, we climb steadily along the edge of the *barranco*, soon joining a broad trail leading to the first houses of **Don Pedro**, from where we have good views over the affluent feeding the waterfall seen at the start of the ascent (Note: the stone pillar passed just before the houses has no great historical significance, but is a replica of an older one that was destroyed). Just after the second house, we join a dirt track (Wp.6 80M).

The **PR-9.2** climbs south towards the **Caldera de Agua** and **La Zarza** (see Walks 19&20) while the GR follows the track into **Don Pedro**, a case of 'No Bar, No Go' as far as we're concerned.

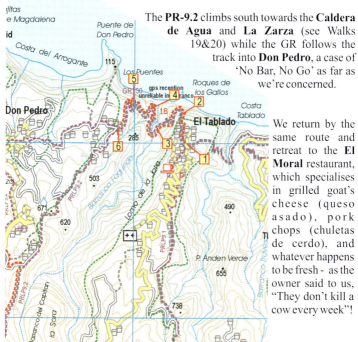

We return by the same route and retreat to the **El Moral** restaurant, which specialises in grilled goat's cheese (queso asado), pork chops (chuletas de cerdo), and whatever happens to be fresh - as the owner said to us, "They don't kill a cow every week"!

The **Caldera de Agua** isn't marked on most maps; the best places never are! The caldera (literally a 'cauldron') is a series of dry waterfalls at the head of the **Barranco de Magdaletín**, hemmed in by the high walls of the ravine and enclosed by a lid of tightly interlacing *laurisilva*. It's a magical place, readily accessible but virtually unknown, and so hushed and tranquil it feels remote.

To reach it we cross a succession of ravines fringed with Canary pine, following drovers' trails and parts of the *pista forestal* that, until a decade ago, constituted the main 'road' between the northern villages (one of the old wooden bridges is still visible from the **LP-1** at the **Barranco Carmona / Cedro** bend, 2.3km east of **La Mata**). And as if that isn't enough, we have the option of a good lunch at **La Mata** restaurant (closed Wednesdays, the kitchen opens at 1pm; specially recommended are the grilled goats cheese, queso asado, marinated goat stew, cabra con salsa, and rabbit with garlic, conejo con ajillo).

NB GPS reception in the *barranco* and calderas after Wp.12 is erratic at best giving potentially false location readings, so there are no waypoints for this stretch of the walk.

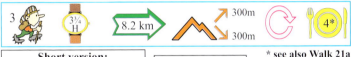

3	3¾ H	8.2 km	⋀	300m / 300m	↻	4*

Short version: Start from **La Mata** (Wp.10)	**Stroll:** Wps.12-16

* see also Walk 21a

The km54 sign at the start of the route

Access by car:
Park on the access road at Wp.1. The walk starts from **Roque del Faro**, opposite the second of the hamlet's three access roads, at km54 of the **LP-1,** 80 metres SW of the bus-stop.

Access by bus:
Via bus N°100 to **Roque del Faro**.The walk starts from **Roque del Faro**, opposite the second of the hamlet's three access roads, at km54 of the **LP-1,** 80 metres SW of the bus-stop.

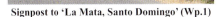
Signpost to 'La Mata, Santo Domingo' (Wp.1)

Opposite the second of **Roque del Faro**'s three access roads, we take a broad concrete track signposted 'La Mata/Santo Domingo' (Wp.1 0M). After descending past a large white building, the concrete gives way to dirt carpeted with pine needles. Winding down to traverse a shallow *barranco*, we join another track (Wp.2 5M) and maintain direction (W), crossing a second shallow *barranco* and the **El Tablado** road (Wp.3 15M).

Curving round the head of **Barranco Carmona**, the track dwindles to an overgrown path, partially cobbled with large black boulders.

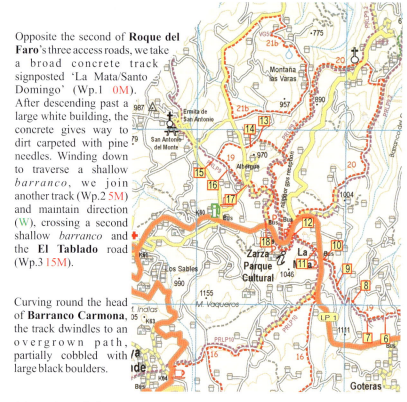

After a short climb on a shady path, we bear right on a grassy track (Wp.4 25M), which turns to deep fine dust as we approach a goat farm. Ignoring a branch to the right, we descend briefly before climbing to a crossroads of dirt tracks (Wp.5 35M).

Continuing straight ahead, we climb to a triple fork (Wp.6 38M). Ignoring tracks to left and right, we follow a narrow, grassy path, signposted 'La Mata/Santo Domingo'. After a short, cobbled descent, the path crosses a deep *barranco* choked with tangled laurel, where it joins another dirt track (Wp.7 40M) and we bear right, climbing above the *barranco*.

We then cross a broader dirt track (Wp.8 45M), part of the old 'road' from the days when the car journey from **Barlovento** to **Garafía** took up to six hours. After a brief descent, we rejoin the 'road' and bear left. We now follow this track all the way to La Mata, passing a path down to the 'Fuente del Capitán' (Wp.9 55M) (30 metres below the track and worth a visit, though not a drink), 150 metres after which we reach the **LP-1** road, just opposite the **Bar/Restaurante La Mata** (Wp.10 58M).

Crossing the road and the car-park behind the restaurant, we take the track for **San Antonio/Santo Domingo** (Wp.11 60M), which dwindles to a path descending to rejoin the road (Wp.12 65M) 50 metres east of the **Zarza Parque Cultural**.

Descending to the small car-park in front of the **Visitors' Centre**, we turn right through a tunnel under the road, signposted 'PR-9.2/9.3 Caldera de Agua/Don Pedro/Santo Domingo'.

One hundred metres from the road, just before several caves, we leave the main trail and bear left on an idyllic woodland path following the bed of a dry stream (75M). Joining a broader path (80M), we bear right for 'Don Pedro/Caldera de Agua' and, 25 metres later, left on a steep, stepped descent into the head of the **Barranco Magdaletín** and the first of three *calderas*.

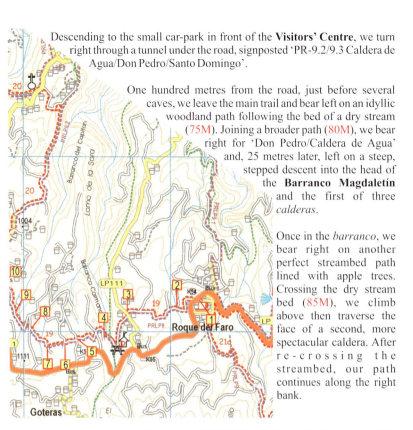

Once in the *barranco*, we bear right on another perfect streambed path lined with apple trees. Crossing the dry stream bed (85M), we climb above then traverse the face of a second, more spectacular caldera. After re-crossing the streambed, our path continues along the right bank.

Ignoring a branch climbing to the right (95M), we descend to the bottom of the heavily wooded *barranco*. We then cross the streambed for the third time (100M) and pass in front of an extraordinary cave set into the base of falls studded with bolted rock handholds.

Fifteen metres after the third crossing, we leave the poorly waymarked PR (which continues down the *barranco*) and turn left on a partially cobbled path that climbs out of the *barranco*. Bearing left at a Y-junction 20 metres later, we climb steeply on a shady path, finally emerging on the level (115M) behind farm buildings, within sight of the antennae-topped **Montaña de San Anton**.

When the path joins the farm track (Wp.13 117M), we bear left and then fork right at a Y-junction 150 metres later (Wp.14 119M). Crossing the **El Mudo/Juan Adalid** road (though you could turn left here and go directly to Wp.17), we follow a dusty dirt track to a signposted T-junction (Wp.15 125M). Turning left for 'La Zarza/Roque del Faro/Roque de los Muchachos' then bearing left again at a Y-junction (Wp.16 27M), we follow a partially cobbled path back to the **El Mudo** road (Wp.17 130M). Crossing the road, we take the narrow tarmac lane directly ahead of us, which we follow back to the **LP-1** road (Wp.18 140M). **La Zarza** is one hundred metres to the left.

We return to Wp.1 via the same route used on the outward leg.

Once you've visited the **Caldera de Agua**, you'll be looking for a pretext to go back, one the local authorities have been good enough to provide in the shape of the **PR-9.2**, a perfect little circuit between **La Zarza** and **Don Pedro**. Short but sweet and, above all, essential walking. GPS reception is unreliable in the ravine, so there are no waypoints after Wp.10.

Access by car:
Park in one of the **Parque Cultural La Zarza** car-parks, either the main car-park on the southern side of the **LP-1** road in front of the *Parque Cultural* or the overflow on the northern side of the road between **La Zarza** and the **Don Pedro** turn-off. The walk starts from the main car-park on the southern side of the road.

Parque Cultural La Zarza

Access by bus:
Bus N°100; alight at the bus-stop which is at **La Zarza** between Wps.1&2

Looking back to Wp.1 from the stone steps

From the main car-park on the southern side of the road (Wp.1 0M), we take the stone steps up onto the **LP-1** and follow the road (NE) past the **Don Pedro** turn-off and bus stop, fifty metres after which we branch left on a narrow tarmac lane (Wp.2 5M).

Less than a minute later, the lane bears right and two dirt tracks branch off to the left (Wp.3 6M); we take the waymarked track that runs alongside the lane. After 300 metres, we rejoin the lane (Wp.4 10M) and follow it as it descends gently. Five metres before the tarmac gives way to dirt, we turn right (NE) on a rough dirt track (Wp.5 15M), which is slippery when damp. At the first Y-junction (Wp.6 20M), we fork left (N then NW), passing two branches on the left before veering north-east again.

When the track bears west (Wp.7 25M), we maintain direction (NNE) on a narrower, grassier trail that brings us in sight of the sea. The trail briefly

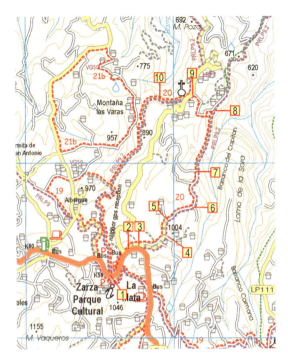

dwindles to an overgrown path before broadening again below an abandoned cabin. Descending a wooded ridge alongside the **Barranco del Capitán** (NNE), we pass a small farmstead where the trail becomes a partially concreted track leading to a tarmac lane (Wp.8 40M).

Turning sharp left, we follow this lane till it joins the **Don Pedro** road. The path to **Don Pedro** continues fifty metres down the road, but we bear left and climb to a small walled shrine, directly above which is the broad path (Wp.9 50M) into the **Caldera de Agua**. Burrowing into the woods with tantalising glimpses of the **Barranco Magdaletín** (N), we pass a small *fuente* with a trough and then a large pool springing from a cleft in the rock (Wp.10 55M).

Zigzagging down into the densely wooded ravine, we cross the watercourse five minutes later and start climbing up the *barranco* (S), sometimes on the left bank, sometimes the right, often following the watercourse itself. Tunnelling under a tangle of tall, thin chestnut and laurel, carpeted with dead leaves, lined with large fern and mossy boulders, and scored with birdsong, this path is a sylvan paradise that ought to be as celebrated as the island's better known routes, but is for the present gloriously neglected.

At the first, long, staired section (65M), we climb steps so badly eroded that they're little more than a ladder of log stair-rods, before dipping down back into the bed of the *barranco*. Continuing up the bed of the *barranco*, we cross a large outcrop of rock (75M), briefly recovering a path on the left bank. Constantly switching back and forth between left and right banks, often as not imperceptibly, we finally come to a narrow stretch between low cliffs mottled with moss and fringed with creepers, after which we pass a small *fuente*/trough/*lavadero* (85M) and join the route of Walk 19 below the *caldera*/waterfall with a cave at its base.

Crossing the stream bed below the first waterfall, we climb steeply on a stepped path (NE) before swinging back to our general southerly direction and passing a large blank mapboard (95M). The path runs alongside the watercourse before re-crossing it and traversing the face of the largest of the three waterfalls. Switching back behind the second falls, we cross the streambed for the third time since joining Walk 19. Emerging from the woods into a broad valley choked with ferns, we pass abandoned apple trees, and stroll along a level path back into shady woodland. The path broadens to a dirt track, which we leave at a Y-junction (105M), bearing right on a waymarked path leading to the third and smallest waterfall.

Turning left in front of the waterfall, we climb to rejoin the dirt track. Bearing right, we follow the track for 25 metres and then branch left on a shady path for **La Zarza**. This delightful sun-dappled path joins another track/trail next to small caves (115M). Bearing right, we pass under the road into the main **La Zarza** car-park, a little way to the west of our starting point.

(a) Barranco de los Hombres

Barranco de los Hombres is one of the largest ravines in the north, an area not notably short of large ravines, but in this gentle stroll, we favour easy walking on the wooded slopes at the head of the *barranco*. What's true of the ravine is true of the *típico*, too. In a region chock-full of fine country restaurants, the **Reyes Restaurante** is outstanding: menu, cuisine and decor are all very simple, but so is the sense of well-being inspired by their rabbit stew (conejo con salsa). Eat in the bar to enjoy the loud bonhomie of local farmers having their midday beer.

Access:

By car or bus N°100. The walk starts in front of the **Reyes Restaurante** on the **LP-1** road, the easternmost access road to **Roque del Faro**, signposted 'PR-9 Los Andenes / Roque de los Muchachos'. There is plenty of room to park near the restaurant.

Reyes Restaurante, Wp.1

Setting off from the **Reyes Restaurante** (Wp.1 0M), we follow the road (S) for 150 metres till it swings right, at which point we maintain direction on a concrete track climbing past an apple orchard. When the concrete gives way to dirt at a Y-junction, we bear left on a partially cobbled track passing a large goat pen.

At the southern end of the goat pen (Wp.2 10M), we branch left on a dirt path descending into an affluent of the **Barranco de los Hombres**. Crossing the bracken filled bed of the affluent, we ignore a clearer path to the left, and turn right on an overgrown, grassy path climbing steeply between mesh fences choked with creepers.

Bearing left when the path joins a minor dirt track, we climb gently (ENE) onto the **Lomo de Rosillo**, the spur separating the affluent from the main ravine. When the track crosses the nose of the spur and starts to descend (Wp.3 20M), we turn right on a broad trail carpeted with pine needles. Climbing gently (S) between huge pine, we pass a path branching left, then join a broad dirt track (Wp.4 25M).

Bearing left, we follow this dirt track into the **Barranco de los Hombres**, ignoring branches to left and right. At a Y-junction (Wp.5 30M), we stay on the main, level branch (right), a delightful forestry track lined with *laurisilva* and towering pine set against a backdrop of the distant rocks on the rim of the *caldera*. A gentle stroll through peaceful woods, serenaded by blackbirds, brings us to a signposted junction, where we bear left, descending on a stretch of concrete to cross the *barranco* (Wp.6 40M).

The **PR-9** turns right immediately after the bridge over the *barranco*, but we stay on the main track, heading northeast, surrounded by superb pine and with good views out to sea. Joining another track at a bend (Wp.7 50M), we bear left. Ignoring all branches, we follow this track down the **Lomo La Rama** (NNW), gradually coming into sight of **Roque del Faro**. We eventually join the old **Barlovento / Mimbreras** road (Wp.8 65M) which also doubles as part of the **PR-9.1**. Bearing left, then left again 100 metres later, we return to our starting point via the main road, which is not nearly so long or steep as it looks from above, and carries very little traffic.

(b) Montaña de las Varas

A pleasant bucolic stroll exploring the countryside above the **Caldera de Agua** (see Walk 19).

*there's a bar, not always open, just after the turning off the main road

Turn north for San Antonio to reach the start

Access by car & (adding two kilometres to the total distance) bus N°100: To reach the start, at km59.7 of the **LP-1** (in sight of the 'Pcan' petrol station), turn north for 'San

The dirt track at our start (Wp.1)

Antonio', setting the odometer at 0. Turn right immediately, as if heading for the coastal hamlet of **Juan Adalid**, then left at the Y-junction after 500 metres.

The walk starts at km 1.1, at a crossroads with a dirt track. There is adequate parking near the junction.

From the junction (Wp.1 0M), we head east along the dirt track, which soon dwindles to a grassy path passing between partially walled pasture and scrub. Ignoring a branch to the left, we reach a U-bend in another dirt track. Bearing right after the U (Wp.2 5M), we follow the track for fifty metres till it swings right, at which point we take a branch track to the left.

Ignoring a branch to the left fifty metres later, we start descending gently on a narrow path tunnelling through the trees. This lovely fairytale path winds down past small potato fields to a join a dirt track (Wp.3 15M), where we bear left and descend toward the sea. Ignoring a branch on the right to the 'PR-9.1 Caldera de Agua/Don Pedro' (Wp.4 20M), we follow the signs for 'Montaña de las Varas', bearing left (NW) below a small farmstead, after which the track narrows and steepens. When the track enters another tree-tunnel section, look out for shallow earth steps to the left (Wp.5 30M). This slip path descends past a small well to rejoin the track twenty metres later.

Bearing left, we follow the track through banks of fern, crossing the **Barranco del Valle**, after which the track swings sharp right, passing a signposted but overgrown path branching left (Wp.6 35M). This path is a shortcut up to our return route, but it probably won't have been cleared (the **SL-50** that used to follow this route appears to have been abandoned), so we stay on the dirt track until we rejoin the **Juan Adalid** lane (Wp.7 45M). From here a steady twenty minute climb up the lane leads back to our starting point.

This was a classic walk long before the **GR-130** was dreamed up and is now one of that path's most popular sections, roller-coasting along like a bucolic theme-ride through the hamlets, farms, and *barrancos* between **Barlovento** and **Gallegos**. The itinerary is well wayposted and can be followed without consulting the book.

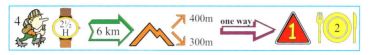

Access by car :
There's ample parking in **Barlovento**. The walk starts at the T-junction at the south-western tip of **Barlovento**.

Access by bus:
Take bus N°100. To reach the start from the **Barlovento** bus stop (which is just above the church) take the main road (the **LP-1** or 'Travesia de Casco Urbano') up through the town for 600 metres.

The walk starts at the T-junction at the south-western tip of **Barlovento**.

Starting at Wp.1

From the T-junction (Wp.1 0M), we follow the **Garafía** road (the **LP-1**) (W). Immediately after a large pale blue house, we leave the main road and bear right (Wp.2 10M), following the **GR-130** as it descends gently on a concrete track, superb views opening out along the undulating coast.

Looking over fine dragon trees to La Tosca

When the concrete gives way to dirt (Wp.3 13M), we bear left on the **Camino Real de Gallegos**, a broad dirt trail crossing a minor *barranco* to the drago-dotted hamlet of **La Tosca** (Wp.4 20M), where we join another concrete track.

Forking left at a Y-junction after 50 metres (a short detour to the right offers close up views of some fine dragon trees), we wind round the mountain to join another concrete track at a U-bend 250 metres later, where we bear right.

After a few minutes, the track swings left (Wp.5 30M) for 'Gallegos' and 'Santo Domingo' and we maintain direction (SW) on a concrete trail that rapidly dwindles to a partially paved path descending into the **Barranco de Topaciegas**. Passing immaculately maintained vegetable patches, we climb steadily onto a spur below a small, partially concealed house with a dragon tree (Wp.6 40M).

When the path joins a concrete track, we bear left and, forty metres later, right on a dirt path (Wp.7 45M) in sight of the **Roque de los Muchachos** observatory. A long, steady descent, takes us across **Barranco de la Vica** (Wp.8 55M) for, no great surprise, a comparably long, steady climb.

Following a broad, very slightly vertiginous path, we climb past an impressive half-dome cave (Wp.9 63M) shortly before reaching the hamlet of **La Palmita**, where we join a concrete track next to two large palm trees (Wp.10 65M).

Maintaining direction (W), we cross the main access track to the hamlet after 160 metres (Wp.11 67M). Carrying straight on, we take a rough, narrow path below a farmhouse, zigzagging down into another mini-*barranco* before climbing steeply to join a dirt track (Wp.12 75M).

Turning right, we cross another concrete track. Heading for the tallest iron pylon, we pass two branch tracks to the left and a huge solitary pine tree, then descend to a signposted path bearing left into the **Barranco de Gallegos** (Wp.13 80M). Going through a gate, we follow a broad dusty goat trail, descending past another very slightly vertiginous stretch, before zigzagging down steeply to the dry bed of the *barranco* (Wp.14 100M).

Following a clear path out of the *barranco*, we climb steeply to a second gateway (Wp.15 110M) before crossing the concrete track (Wp.16 120M) leading to the hamlet of **La Crucita**, already within sight of **Gallegos**.

Zigzagging down past wild tomato plants, we cross the final *barranco*, passing a row of troglodytic cabins before climbing to a small plaza in the village (Wp.17 130M), where there's a taxi stand and unmarked bus stop (bus Nº100).

30 metres down the street is the **Bar Viveres**, which doubles as a mini-market. If there's time, it's worth exploring the village before catching the bus back to **Barlovento**.

Bar Viveres

Despite a disproportionate amount of walking on concrete and tarmac, this little known circuit is a delightful introduction to the countryside around **Barlovento**, particularly the rich variety of trees that the region enjoys.

Apart from one steep climb, the walking is easy, making this an ideal route for relaxing after some of our more energetic itineraries. The access and start are the same as for Walk 22, the first eleven waypoints of which have been incorporated into the waypoint file for this itinerary.

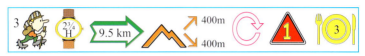

Access: by car or bus Nº100 (see Walk 22 for details)

We start by following the **GR-130** and Walk 22 to Wp.11 (67M), where we turn left on the hamlet access track, climbing along the **SL-LP40** and passing a magnificent dragon tree before joining the main road 400 metres later (Wp.12 80M). Bearing left, we follow the road for 900 metres into the **Barranco de la Vica**, where we turn right on a dirt track signposted 'SL-LP40 Barlovento' (Wp.13 90M).

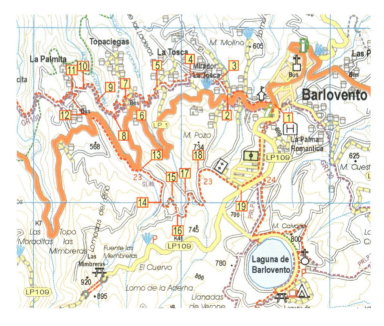

The track climbs gently then steadily between the steepening walls of the *barranco*, flanked by shady heath, chestnut and laurel trees, sheltering throngs of songbirds. 30 metres before a small cliff (Wp.14 100M), we leave the dirt track and turn left to climb a steep, narrow, signposted path (see photo on next page) that crosses a water canal. Ignoring a trail descending to the

Our steep, signposted path (Wp.14)

right a minute or so above the canal, we continue to climb steeply along a shady path with occasional earth steps. Passing behind a ruin, we join the end of a grassy track (Wp.15 105M).

At the top of the track, we bear right on a concrete track, then left when this in turn joins a major dirt track (Wp.16 115M) in sight of **Montaña del Pozo** (on our left). Enjoying fine views of green hills backed by blue sea, we stroll past bushy laurel, heather, fern, the odd wild gladioli, pear trees and a cascade of blackberries.

Fine views after Wp.16

Forking right (Wp.17 125M) then left at successive Y-junctions, we follow the intermittently metalled track as it snakes round the head of **Barranco de Topaciegas** before climbing gently to a large green building (Wp.18 140M).

Turning right and continuing on the main track, we ignore branches into the surrounding fields, and pass a cemetery, after which (still on **SL-LP40**) we take the cemetery lane up toward the **Barlovento / Las Mimbreras** road (Wp.19 147M).

Turning left 15 metres before the main road, we follow a broad pavement alongside an industrial zone for 300 metres until the **SL-LP40** joins the **PR-LP8** (Wp.20 150M). Following the **PR-LP8** downhill, we pass a football ground, then cross the **Mimbreras** road twice, the first time onto a dirt track that soon dwindles to a path, the second time onto a grassy track that rejoins the road seventy-five metres from our starting point.

On the whole, people responsible for PRs & GRs tend to stick to time-honoured trails, following old transhumance routes, royal ways and logging tracks, but here the pathmakers have done us proud, trailblazing a superb little path through the woods above **Barranco de la Herradura**, to give us a linear route through a typically and uniquely La Palman combination of tropical forest, misty heathland and tiny fields squeezed into the encroaching forest. There are fine views en route, though in all probability, these will be shrouded in cloud. Fortunately, the path is quite pretty enough of itself, whether you see anything beyond it or not.

4   3¾ H   11.5 km   400m / 650m   one way   4

Access: see Walks 22 & 23. The walk starts on a grassy track 75 metres above the **LP-1/LP-109** roads T-junction, between the **Conjunto Residencial Tajinaste** and signs for the football field and cemetery.

> ### Short Circular Version
>
> Follow the main route to Wp.5 then take the **PR-LP7.1** to the left, crossing **Lomo Chico** to pick up the **GR-130**, which we follow back to our start at Wp.1 - distance 6.5km.

Wp.1 - the start of the route

Setting off on the grassy track 75 metres above the **Garafía** turn-off (the same track used at the end of Walk 23) (Wp.1 0M), we climb steadily, crossing the **Mimbreras** road twice, the first time onto a path that broadens to a dirt track, the second onto a back road climbing past the football ground.

Rejoining the road at a 'PR-8/SL-40' signpost (Wp.2 20M), we turn left then, fifty metres later, right on a concrete track. The track curves through a U-bend and we branch right on the second of two dirt tracks, which we follow till it joins the *laguna* road (Wp.3 30M). Leaving the **PR-8**, we turn left and follow the road up to the *laguna*.

If doing the full walk, you may wish to stay on the road round the *laguna* rather than take the following short but strenuous detour, in which case cut fifteen minutes from the overall time. Otherwise, turn left at the *laguna* on stone steps up to a small *mirador*. From the *mirador*, a dirt track runs parallel to the road, climbing steadily then steeply to the 800 metre trig point on **Montaña del Calvario** (Wp.4 40M), where we continue on a narrow path burrowing through vegetation to join a clearer path. Bearing left, we follow this path down to a dirt track, where we turn right and descend back to the *laguna*, just north of the open-air chapel / *plaza* (Wp.5 50M) used to celebrate local festivals.

Ignoring the 'Los Sauces PR-7.1', we stay on the *laguna* road, passing the campsite, where there's a bar/restaurant. At the end of the metalled road, we bear right on a broad dirt path, the 'Los Tilos PR-7.1' (Wp.6 55M), climbing roughly-hewn steps.

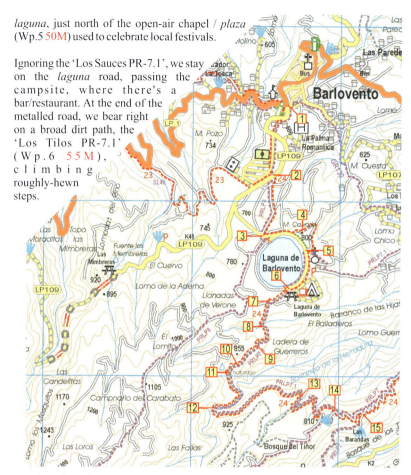

Ignoring a branch track to the right, we join a broad dirt track, fifty metres along which we turn left (Wp.7 60M), still following the 'Los Tilos' signposts. The track dips into **Barranco de las Hijas**, where we turn left (Wp.8 75M) on a stepped path under an immense walnut tree. After a steep climb we join a narrow dirt track beside an apple orchard. Turning right and then left 75 metres later, we pass between the apple orchard and a plum orchard, before bearing right at a Y-junction (Wp.9 85M). A steady climb past a melon patch leads to a small clearing and a signposted path descending SW (Wp.10 90M).

The path, fenced with rough railings, descends the steep, densely forested **Ladera de Guerreros** into the first complex folds of the **Barranco de la Herradura**, crossing a footbridge below an ochre-stained spring mottled with lichen (Wp.11 95M). Climbing away from the spring, we pass the first of two wickerwork cabin frames, before descending again, negotiating a few metres where the railings have collapsed and the path is crumbling away. Following the folds of the *barranco*, we cross a *galería* pipe, passing a large works hut (Wp.12 110M) and a source tunnel.

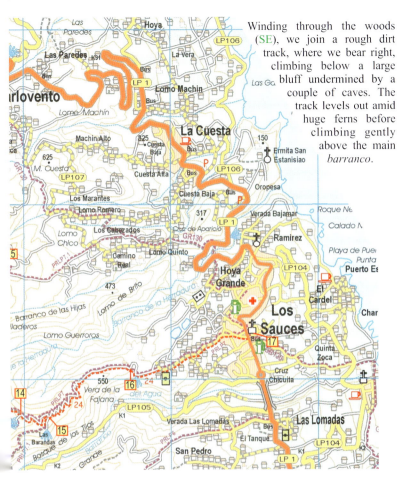

Winding through the woods (SE), we join a rough dirt track, where we bear right, climbing below a large bluff undermined by a couple of caves. The track levels out amid huge ferns before climbing gently above the main *barranco*.

Passing in and out of shade, we wind round watersheds and affluent gullies, crossing a small mudslide where the track narrows to a path (Wp.13 135M), finally joining the **PR-7** *pista forestal* from **Pico de la Cruz** (Wp.14 150M).

Turning left ,we follow this track virtually all the way to **Los Sauces**, ignoring all but two branches, the first being the turning for **Mirador de las Baranda** or **del Topo de la Baranda** (Wp.15 160M), a five minute excursion from the main track and well worth it if the **Barranco del Agua and Los Tilos** aren't under cloud. Returning to the main track we continue our descent, again ignoring all branches until we pass a large camouflaged reservoir, shortly after which we bear right (Wp.16 190M) on a steep, well-paved shortcut, rejoining the track at another *mirador* a few minutes later. Maintaining direction (E), we pass a large antenna and descend steeply toward **Los Sauces**, first on concrete then on tarmac. In the built up area, we follow the main tarmac lane down to the town square (Wp.17 210M).

The bus stop is to the left, next to the church, the taxi stand to the right on the western side of the square.

25 LOS TILOS

In one form or another, this is a 'must-do' for every visitor to La Palma. Setting off from the **Casa del Monte** (1280 metres), we follow the **Los Tilos** canal round the head of the **Barranco Rivero** (later **del Agua**) to the **Marcos** and **Cordero** springs, traversing 13 tunnels en route. We then descend the ravine through the jungle-like **Tilos** forest to the **Visitors' Centre** access road. And for once, 'descent' does not imply diminishing returns. Every step of the way, we are surprised by constantly unfolding and improving views, while the *laurisilva* forest gets deeper, denser and greener to the very end. Not for a moment does it disappoint and I strongly recommend the full walk, though the short versions both qualify as 'must-dos', too.

The only drawback is that the full walk involves taking a 4x4 taxi and having your own car (or another taxi) at the end. The dirt track from **Las Lomadas** to **Casa del Monte** (signposted 'Nacimientos de Marcos y Cordero' in the village, thereafter 'Casa del Monte') is often passable without 4x4 and though lightweight, short-wheelbase cars might make it, rental cars aren't insured for off-road driving, so we can't recommend driving there yourself.

Although we follow a canal perched high above the ravine, the risk of vertigo is minimal, as the path is wide and the most vertiginous sections are fenced with railings. In fact, the tunnels mean there's a bigger

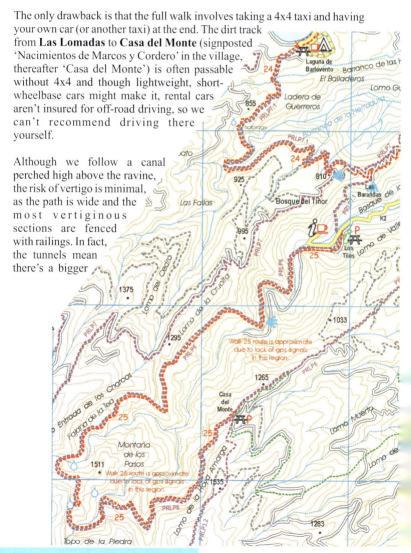

risk of claustrophobia than vertigo. That said, do not (this isn't a joke, you'd be surprised how many people do this) lean over railings to 'get a good photo' of yourself. There's a risk of rock slides after or during heavy rains. The only other danger is the obvious one of clouting your head on low tunnel roofs. A TORCH IS ESSENTIAL as some of the tunnels are very long and very dark. Also A WATERPROOF CAPE IS STRONGLY RECOMMENDED as it's raining in tunnel number twelve - all the time, very heavily. Italic numbers after walking times are the minutes required to traverse longer tunnels. Short tunnels are given no traverse time.

The water in the canal is for drinking, so no dipping in to refresh yourself on a hot day. The short walk to **Mirador de Espigón Atravesado** is easy though the *mirador* itself is very vertiginous.

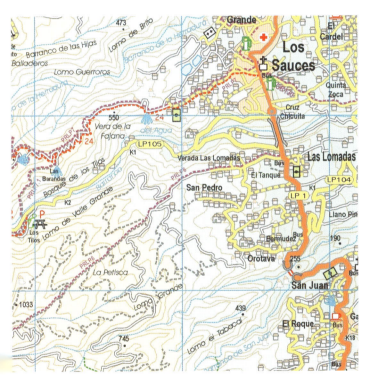

NB Due to poor GPS reception, no waypoints are given for this itinerary, but the route is well waymarked and obvious.

** allow 4-5 hours   *** at the Visitors' Centre**

Access: 4x4 taxi and car
The 4x4 taxi service is pricey and there have been reports of drivers charging

over the odds. However, shared taxis make the trip considerably cheaper, in the order of €30 per couple. Rather than printing information that risks becoming out of date, we recommend visiting the nearest Tourist Information Office and asking them to phone the **Los Sauces** and **Los Tilos** taxi rank (922 450 928) for up-to-date information on who's offering the 4x4 service to 'Casa del Monte' and what the prices are. The Tourist Information Office will also be able to tell you if anyone offers a 4x4 taxi service local to wherever you're staying. For obvious reasons, shared and therefore cheaper taxis are easier to come by in the summer and at weekends. Arrange to meet your driver at the end of the **PR-6**, km2.4 of the Visitors' Centre access road (the **LP-105**), where there's a lay-by, mapboard, and small car-park. If you're staying nearby, it's worthwhile popping into the **Visitors' Centre** at the end of the **LP-105** the day before.

The canal and Casa del Monte at the start

The walk starts just west of the **Casa del Monte** (a pleasant picnic spot, worth visiting while you get your bearings), at the junction of the **PR-3.2** and **PR-6** (0M). We take the broad canal path (SW), signposted 'Entrada por El Canal à Marcos y Cordero 4.5km 13 túneles'.

Winding alongside the canal with *laurisilva* 'blinkers' to our right, we glimpse **Barranco Rivero** through the trees before rounding a bend to a stretch of railings and our first superb views across the ravine.

Tunnel Nº1 (8M *3M*) is easy at first as we walk on top of the canal, but gets lower halfway along, obliging us to drop down alongside the canal. After the much shorter and easier Tunnel Nº2 (17M), we reach a slightly vertiginous section with railings, beyond which views open out behind us down the *barranco* to its confluence with the **Cordero** watercourse. Tunnel Nº3 (24M *8M*), which has a small cave at its mouth, is the longest and most intimidating you certainly wouldn't want to bump into anything hairy down there! After 30 metres, puddles appear underfoot and the roof dips down. The tunnel gets lower and tighter as the canal wall gets higher.

Finally, we glimpse daylight, but have to bend over sideways, possibly even taking off a bulky rucksack, as the roof slopes further in. We eventually emerge on a small ledge and immediately duck into the short but very low Tunnel Nº4. Crossing a bridge over a small ravine, we come to Tunnel Nº5 (38M). At first the way is reasonably well lit by windows, but soon darkens and narrows, forcing us to squeeze between the tunnel wall and canal, before emerging briefly then ducking into Tunnel Nº6 (43M), which, like its predecessor, is about 75 metres long. Tunnels Nºs 7 & 8 (45M & 48M), are short and require no torch.

Tunnel Nº9 (49M) is longer, but reasonably lit. It narrows halfway along, forcing us to bend double and walk on the canal wall. Back in the open, we descend round a holding tank before continuing on a narrow, railed path. Tunnel Nº10 (57M) is short, but curves so we need the torch. Tunnel Nº11 (59M) is well lit by windows and soon emerges on a narrow railed balcony, where we hear the roar of water and see the waterfall lined path climbing above the **Nacimiento de Marcos**.

Tunnel Nº12 (61M) is where we don our waterproofs. This may seem prissy, but it's raining in there, heavily, so it's either waterproofs or duck and run. You may find plastic bin bags here, though that depends on which way the last group went. Climbing over a small sluice gate onto a narrow overflow path, we go through the rain, pausing if it's not too cold to enjoy the view through windows curtained by sheets of water.

We now pass the **Marcos** source and climb steeply on deep stone steps alongside the roaring waters descending from the Cordero. After a second, slightly less steep climb on stone steps, we join the **Cordero** canal (71M). Strolling along the canal, we come to our last tunnel, Nº13 (74M), which looks easy but is studded with head clouting protuberances. We soon hear roaring water again as we approach the **Nacimiento de Cordero** (80M) where we begin our descent.

Bearing right, a steep, stepped descent brings us down to the dry **Cordero** watercourse, where we cross a rock-spill to pass the signposted junction with the **SL-30**, a path which even the Spanish say is 'very dangerous' (85M). Our path drops down, switching onto the right bank of the watercourse, which falls away to our left. Gradually descending through pine to the denser *laurisilva*, we re-cross the watercourse (90M). After passing a second dangerous-path, another of the many stepped descents brings us back into the bed of the *barranco* (95M), which we follow for the next fifteen minutes.

Hopping from boulder to boulder and levering ourselves down water-chutes, we descend between cliffs cloaked with moss, ivy, houseleeks and shrubby *laurisilva*. After ten minutes, we come to a narrower section where a trodden dirt path winds through the boulders and debris of fallen trees passing marvellous giant ferns (105M, see photo on next page).

The *barranco* broadens slightly and we come to a waypost, where we bear right before crossing a footbridge (110M) back onto the *barranco*'s left bank, which we follow on a good dirt path for most of the descent down the wooded slopes of the **Fajana de la Tea**.

Boulders and giant ferns at 105 minutes

Alternating level stretches and descents, during which the watercourse drops away steeply below us and views open out across the *barranco*, lead to a broad fenced ledge forming a natural *mirador* (115M), after which we pass a slightly vertiginous section before crossing the first of several affluent watersheds.

The forest gradually closes in and we begin our final, steep descent, passing a small, stagnant *fuente* (135M). The descents continue and the further down we go the deeper the forest becomes. The path finally swings right to cross a footbridge over the **Barranco del Agua** (150M), beyond which a brief climb brings us onto a broad dirt trail, where we bear left.

This trail is a delight, winding down the valley on a beautifully mottled carpet of dead leaves, tunnelling through towering trees festooned with hanging creepers, and passing ferns so huge they dwarf even the giants seen higher up the ravine. We soon come to the **Mirador de Espigón Atravesado** location board (160M). You'll understand why the board's not actually on the *mirador* if you take the stepped branch on the right just after the board, a five minute diversion (counted in subsequent timings) that I strongly recommend. The branch path weaves between railings and thin walls of rock along an incredibly narrow ridge till it reaches the *mirador*, a tiny fenced ledge (room for about 4 people who really like each other) suspended above nothing.

After visiting the *mirador*, we simply follow the main trail back to the **Los Tilos** access road, passing a small cabin swallowed by vegetation (175M) and an information board (185M) about the Til or Greenheart tree that gives the reserve its name. After going through a 'train' tunnel, we bear left and descend to the parking area (195M).

The **Barranco de la Galga**, popularly known as the 'Cubo' or bucket, is a smaller version of **Los Tilos**, a stunning gorge packed with spectacular primeval forest so exceptional that it has been incorporated into the biosphere reserve. Better still, recent developments have improved what was already a classic hike into a near perfect circuit with excellent parking facilities and a bus-stop at the trail-head.

Beautiful shady forest, birdsong, and the soothing sound of water dripping from the rocks make the **Cubo** an absolute haven, one that is particularly welcome after exposure to the sun on the island's higher, drier itineraries. A pamphlet about the 'Sendero Autoguiado' or 'self-guided path' that we use to begin with may be obtained from the information hut at the start (if it's manned, which is not always the case).

NB Poor GPS reception due to the geology of the gorge means there are no waypoints given in the text after Wp.2

* **and ** ** time and distance vary depending on which optional return is chosen**

The stone sign marks our start

Access by bus:
Bus Nº100 runs between **Los Llanos - Santa Cruz**. The walk starts at km16.1 of the **LP-1** road between two tunnels, where there is a bus stop, car park, a prominent 'Cubo de la Galga' stone sign and an information hut.

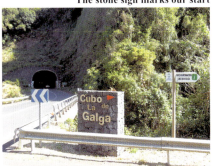

Access by car:
Take the **LP-1** road to km 16.1 between two tunnels, where there is a bus stop, car park, a prominent 'Cubo de la Galga' stone sign, and an information hut.

From the information hut (Wp.1 0M), we take the **Sendero Autoguiado** (marked by green-waymarked wooden posts), which follows a surfaced lane into the *barranco* (SW). At a left bend, we pass the end of one of our return routes (the 'agricultural' option - see below), a branch climbing to the left for 'La Galga' (Wp.2 3M). Staying on the lane for now, we climb steadily, passing impressive cliffs, after which chestnut trees and *laurisilva* crowd in on either side. After a little over a kilometre, the tarmac gives way to dirt (15M) and our steady climb is interrupted by a succession of brief level stretches, from one of which we see a high cliff to the south pierced by *galería* 'windows' along the **Canal del Estado**. Passing under an aqueduct (23M), we continue our steady climb, crossing and re-crossing the watercourse several times until we reach a junction in a left bend (35M).

A short detour to the right will take us into an impressive valley basin where there's a refreshing waterfall. To reach the waterfall, when the branch track ends three minutes from the junction, push through the dense blackberry shrubs to the overhanging cliff, below which (depending upon the season) we can enjoy an improvised shower.

Otherwise, at the junction, we bear left to continue on the main itinerary. When this track also ends 130 metres later, we take the log steps onto the main forest path through the **Cubo**. 50 metres after passing under an aqueduct, we come to a T-junction where we join the **PR-LP5.1** (39M). Our 'forest' return route (see below) feeds in from the left here, but we turn right for 'Mirador de Somada Alta' and climb steadily on log steps.

The aqueduct

The trail, which is intermittently protected by railings and occasionally runs through muddier sections, climbs steadily, then winds up and down through dense woodland above the seemingly bottomless *barranco*.

Shortly after crossing a shallow dry river bed, we climb to join a broad dirt track (56M) where we turn sharp left for the 'Mirador de Somada Alta'.

Following the track (NE), we climb gently for one kilometre to a small clearing where our trail joins the **PR-LP 5** (74M).

The junction at 39 minutes

The **Mirador de Somada Alta**, a curiously elaborate structure of step, tunnel and terrace lies off to our left. We can either go under the footbridge to join our way down immediately or cross the footbridge and descend to the dilapidated mapboard at the *mirador*'s tip (75M) before doubling back on the lower terrace to join the path down to **La Galga**.

Either way, we now follow the **PR-LP5** and **5.1** on a path that zigzags down from the south-eastern tip of the *mirador* (E) alongside a silver water pipe in a deep trench-like cutting. When the path runs into a narrow dirt track in a meadow, we maintain direction along the forest edge, at first on the narrow track, then back in the trench-trail again. After a steep descent, following the water pipe throughout, we emerge below a house on a concrete driveway beside a junction (91M). Turning left at the junction, we take another concrete lane (NW), following the **PR-LP5.1** for 'Cubo de La Galga' and 'San

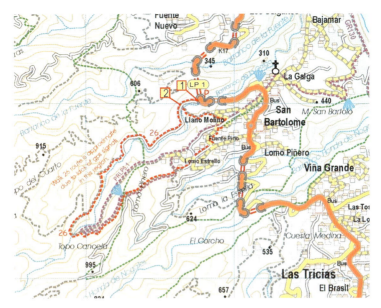

Bartolome'. Five minutes later, we reach a mapboard and a signpost next to a small water station (96M).

We now have two options for returning to the start, the first remaining in the deep forest but repeating the first 40 minutes of the outward leg, the second more varied option traversing an agricultural landscape and only coinciding with the outward route for the last few minutes.

Option 1, the forest route: turning left at the water station (SW), we follow a path that runs along a canal then climbs steadily before finally dropping back to the **Cubo de la Galga** T-junction at the 39M point, from where we follow the outward route back to the car park.

Option 2, the agricultural route: turning right at the water station (NE), we continue on the concrete lane which soon becomes a broader tarmac lane passing a majestic solitary pine.

A few minutes later, when a water pipe runs under a patched stretch of tarmac, we leave the lane and bear left onto a footpath (102M). Following the water pipe, we descend to a concrete lane beside the driveway to a house. Carrying straight on in the same direction (NE) and ignoring two branches off to the right, we continue to follow the water pipe along the lane, until we come to a T-junction with a broader, heavily patched lane (111M), where we bear left below elevated water pipes. The lane immediately bends to the right.

After 30 metres, at a light-green house, we turn left onto a covered canal (signposted 'Punto de Información'), the entrance to which is obscured by the spreading branches of a tree (112M). 100 metres later, we leave the canal and descend to the right onto a footpath. One minute later, we cross a water pipe onto concrete stairs, beyond which the path plunges back into the forest. Descending steeply, we rejoin the tarmac lane at the **La Galga** turn off (126M) where we turn right to return to our starting point (131M).

Once you've driven up to the **Roque de los Muchachos** (The Lads' Rock, the highest point on the island) and done your obligatory gasping, you may question the attractions of trudging along the barren rim of the *caldera*. But pottering about in a car-park can never match walking to give a sense of place and every new approach to the rim is an eye-opener. This short itinerary, which never strays far from the road, is one of those rare walks that are easy yet take you through decidedly uneasy terrain. If walking in winter, wrap up warm. In summer, sunscreen and a hat are essential. Not recommended in wet or windy weather. There's a very slight risk of vertigo.

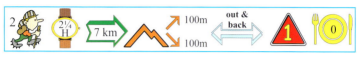

Access by car:
The walk starts at km31.2 of the **LP-4 Santa Cruz - Hoya Grande** road, where there's a signpost for 'Pico de la Cruz **PR-7/8**'. There are several roadside parking spaces to the east of Wp.1.

From km31.2 of the **LP-4** (Wp.1 0M), we set off on the **Pico de la Cruz PR7/8** route, climbing a paved stairway that almost immediately joins the **GR-131 Ruta de la Crestería** (Wp.2 1M).

The main walk is to the right, but it's worth turning left first, either to visit the natural *mirador* at the end of the

Our start at the paved stair (Wp.1)

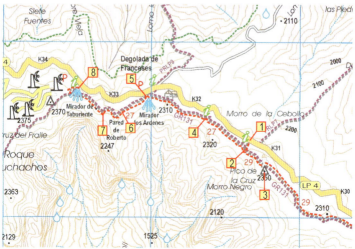

trodden path ten metres from the junction, or to follow the GR up to **Pico de la Cruz** (Wp.3 10M) for superb views over the *caldera* and across the sea of clouds to Tenerife, La Gomera and El Hierro. Returning to the **GR-131/PR-7** junction, we pick our way (W) across waymarked rocks onto a clear path climbing behind a small rise. Descending toward the road, we pass a signpost for the 'Barranco del Diablo' and 'Barranco de Gallegos' (Wp.4 30M), then climb a shallow broom-covered slope, passing a junction, before re-descending to the road at the **Degollada de Los Franceses**.

Following the road for 30 metres, we reach **Mirador de los Andenes** (Wp.5 45M), where we recover a narrow dirt

Pared de Roberto

Mirador de los Andenes

path. From a distance, this path appears to cross a sheer red slope before petering out. In fact, it's not nearly so alarming as it looks from afar. The point at which it appears to peter out is the gateway through the **Pared de Roberto** (Wp.6 47M), one of the natural basaltic walls that are such a distinctive feature of the **Caldera**.

Legend has it that a young man used to cross the *cumbre* to visit his girlfriend. Jealous of their love, the devil, who seems to have spent a lot of time gadding about these parts, manifested himself as 'Roberto' and threw up this 'insurmountable' wall, blocking the young man's path. 'Roberto' then proposed a Faustian pact, making a gateway in exchange for his victim's soul. To be honest, our hapless lover was either no great climber or prized his soul over-lightly, but the deal was done and the gateway remains.

… a distinctive three-headed rock spire …

After the gateway, we continue along the GR, climbing before dropping down to another natural *mirador* (Wp.7 60M). We then cross another small rise and, less 100 metres after a distinct three-headed rock spire, turn right to a board with a hand-drawn map of the *caldera* (Wp.8 70M).

Unless possessed of a compelling urge to climb to a car-park, we return the same way.

This is the rugged end of the crater and, in pure walking terms, perhaps the most interesting stretch of path on the rim, winding between rocks, dipping up and down, changing all the time, and eventually climbing to a unique outlook on the island's question mark spine.

4 | 1¾ H | 6 km | 300m 300m | out & back | 0

The start of the route

Access by car:
The walk starts at km2.9 of the **Observatory** access road, a little over 500 metres west of **Roque de los Muchachos**, on a dirt track branching south. There's parking for three cars next to the map-board of the descent to **Torre del Time**. If the parking area is full, continue up to the **Roque de**

On the dirt track after Wp.1, the Observatory visible

los Muchachos car park then walk back to the starting point following the **GR-131**.

From the road (Wp.1 0M), we follow the dirt track for a few metres before bearing right on the broad, **GR-131** waymarked path we will follow to the base of **Roque Palmero**. The path runs parallel to the dirt track before passing two drum-like satellite dishes and bearing west to a small weather-hut. We then pass a sign for the 'Barrancos de Hoyo Verde' and 'Izcagua', and skirt round the base of **Roque Chico** (Wp.2 10M).

We now descend to a signpost for the 'Barranco de Marangaño' (Wp.3 15M), just before which it's worth bearing left a few metres to a natural *mirador* over-looking the crater towards La Gomera. Returning to the GR, a short, steady climb crosses a craggy, unnamed peak, after which we skirt behind a larger bluff, the **Morro de la Crespa** (Wp.4 20M).

Crossing a small rise backed by a broad firebreak, we pass a stubby, battered geodesic survey post (Wp.5 30M), from where we have superb views into the **Barranco de Bombas de Agua**, flanked by small basaltic walls you'd swear were man-made, and enough shades of brown to shame a Flemish Old Master.

A rough, rocky descent brings us down to the **Degollada de las Palomas** (Wp.6 35M) dividing the **Barrancos de Bombas de Agua** and **de Garome**.

Continuing in a southerly direction, we cross four outcrops of rock, the first relatively large and topped by boulders, the second no more than a thin angled shelf poking through the path.

Immediately after the outcrops we leave the GR, turning left on a faint trodden way marked by two large cairns and a GR cross (Wp.7 40M). The cairn-marked way climbs steadily, weaving through the scrub to the trig point on the very rocky **Roque Palmero** (Wp.8 50M), from where we have good views over the **Caldera** and **Cumbres Nueva and Vieja**.

We return via the same route, resisting the temptation to take a slip path round the nameless peak south of Wp.3 (narrow path, steep slope, abrupt drop = flat head!).

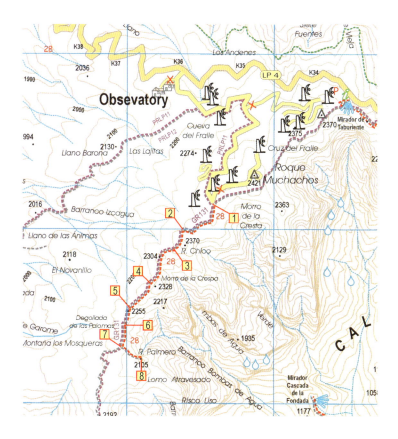

This stretch of the **Caldera**'s rim is perhaps the most photogenic and many postcards, notably early morning shots of the crater full of cloud, are taken from the photo-spots mentioned in the text. Following the **GR-131**, we wind round the small peaks of the north-eastern rim, peering into deep *barrancos* defined by narrow pinnacles of rock, and gazing at the vari-coloured strata underpinning the lip of the crater. Given that this is a linear walk, short versions can be readily improvised, but logical turning points would be Wp.5 or Wp.6.

Access: see Walk 27

We start as in Walk 27, at km 31.2 of the **LP-4 Santa Cruz - Hoya Grande** road, on the paved stairway beside the **PRs 7&8** mapboard, signposted 'Pico de la Cruz PR7/8' (Wp.1 0M). After climbing onto the **GR-131** (Wp.2 1M),

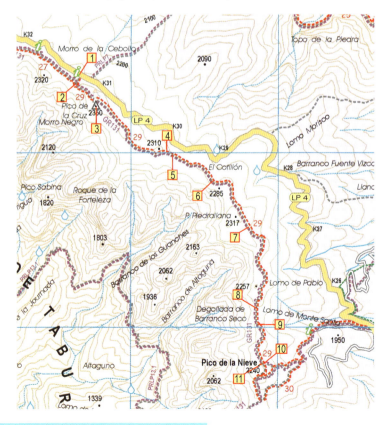

Descending from Pico de la Cruz

we bear left for a short, steady ascent to **Pico de la Cruz** (Wp.3 10M). From the peak, we descend (E) across a rock-filled hollow onto a clear dirt path winding along the crest towards a distant 'agave' sculpture.

Views to Mount Teide (Wps 6-7)

Skirting a small rise, we briefly lose sight of the crater, before climbing onto a second small rise topped with a rocky outcrop (Wp.4 25M), immediately after which, we pass the first photo-spot (Wp.5 26M).

Winding along a section where the narrow rim is sandwiched between the road and the crater, we pass the second photo-spot (Wp.6 35M). Neither are physically distinct, but the views are all the identification they require.

We then climb gently, passing a dilapidated signpost for 'Barranco de los Guanches' (in the crater) and 'Barranco de la Fuente Vizcaino' (E). After passing a little way below the peak's trig point, we reach a sign for 'Pico Piedrallana' (Wp.7 45M), from where we have stunning views over the **Barranco de Altaguna**.

Our path now zigzags down over light volcanic rock to the first of two watersheds feeding the *barranco*. We then skirt the small top separating us from the second, signposted watershed, where there's also a sign for 'Barranco de Altaguna' (in the crater) and 'Barranco Hondo' (E) (Wp.8 65M). Climbing between large boulders, we pass a distinctive oblong block of rock, shortly after which a trodden way bears right to a natural *mirador* (Wp.9 70M).

Pico de la Nieve at Wp.11

Continuing on the main path, we skirt behind the small **Pico del Cedro**, after which the **GR-131** joins the **PR-LP3** (Wp.10 78M). A short, easy climb to the right brings us to the summit cross of **Pico de la Nieve** (Wp.11 80M). We return via the same route.

This easy route on clear paths is one of the few practical ascents of the **Caldera** to give a sense of actually climbing somewhere, most of the other ways to the top either being too short to count or too long for comfort. The outlook across the crater is all the better for being reached on foot. The usual recommendations apply: cover up as befits the season and beware of the wind the summit is very exposed.

At the start

Access:
By car. We start at km24.9 of the **LP-4 Santa Cruz -Roque de los Muchachos** road, at the junction with the *pista forestal* to 'Pico de la Nieve'. Park on the southern side of the track for shade.

Taking the **PR-LP 3** (Wp.1 0M) just north of the *pista forestal* 'Pico de la Nieve'), we climb long, shallow steps alongside the road before

switching back on a gentler slope through the pine woods, where the path becomes a broad trail marked with regular cairns, climbing steadily to the turning circle at the end of the *pista forestal* (Wp.2 20M).

Staying behind the turning circle, we take the path above the *pista*, passing a mapboard and crossing a dry watercourse. Climbing steadily again, we pass a small wooden cross with a corroded commemorative plaque (Wp.3 25M), then turn right at a signposted junction (Wp.4 30M) for 'Pico de la Nieve / Roque de los Muchachos'.

Climbing through the last scattered pine to the broom covered slopes below the peak, we come into sight of Santa Cruz, the **Cumbre Vieja**, Tenerife and La Gomera, then El Hierro, and finally the southern part of the crater and **Pico Bejenado**. Joining the **GR-131** (Wp.5 50M) on the crest, we turn right to reach a signposted junction (Wp.6 53M), where we bear left to reach the summit cross on the bleak, windswept **Pico de la Nieve** (Wp.7 55M).

Retracing our steps to the **GR-131/PR-3** junction, we head south along the crest, passing a small natural windbreak. The GR descends on a rocky path partially overgrown with broom, passing behind a small rise onto a more densely overgrown but still discernible stretch leading to the junction with our return route (Wp.8 70M), signposted 'Pista Pico de la Nieve/Salida'.

NB An interesting detour to the right here (20 minutes return, not counted in subsequent or global timings), brings us to the **Tagoror** petroglyphs and a great viewing point on **Pico de la Sabina**.

Pico de la Sabina

Otherwise, we turn left on a narrow path that descends gently then follows the contours of the mountain with fine views over **Santa Cruz**, rejoining our outward route at Wp.4 (80M), from where we can either follow the same path back to the start, or descend via the dirt track after Wp2.

The **Cumbrecita** is at the end of the only asphalted road into the **Caldera** (other than the narrow lane into the **Barranco de las Angustias** - see Walk 33) and is popular with sightseers, so get there early - by 10 o'clock so many cars are shunting back and forth it resembles the lower deck of a ferry. Don't be discouraged, though. This short walk is an excellent introduction to the interior of the **Caldera**, taking us past a series of pictorial information boards explaining the crater's formation and ecology.

Due to repeated problems with landslides, the vertiginous and frequently dangerous continuation of the canal path (north of Wp.8) that approaches the park campsite via the **Galería de Aridane**, **Hoyo de los Pinos**, and **Lomo de Escuchadero** is most emphatically not recommended.

The higher Cumbrecita car park (Wp.1)

Access by car:
NB access to **La Cumbrecita** is restricted and you must call in at the **Caldera de Taburiente Visitors' Centre** (just east of the junction of the **LP-2** and **LP-202**) to collect an Access Number that will be checked en route to the start via the **Carretera Cumbrecita**.

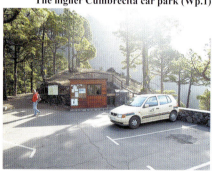

The walk begins in the higher of the two **Cumbrecita** car-parks at the end of the road.

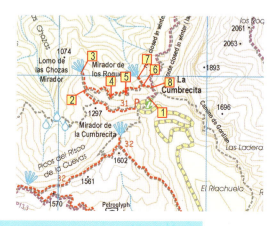

.. take a broad dirt track ..

Setting off from the higher **Cumbrecita** car-park (Wp.1 0M), we cross the lower car-park and take a broad dirt track (W), which we follow all the way to the **Lomo de las Chozas** *mirador*.

Strolling along and pausing to inspect the ceramic information boards, we pass the **Mirador de los Roques** path doubling back on the right (Wp.2 15M). Continuing along the track to circle the 'island' at the end of the *lomo*, we descend to the *mirador* (Wp.3 20M), where we have excellent views of **Lomo de los Bueyes**.

Returning to Wp.2, we descend gently on a narrow path, the vegetation around us an object lesson in the flora panels seen on the track. After crossing two footbridges (Wps.4&5 35M & 40M), we climb two brief flights of steps to join the canal path (Wp.6 45M), where we bear left to **Mirador de los Roques** (Wp.7 47M). The views from here are even better and we can pick out the thin silver thread of the **Cascada de la Fondada** (NW) above the broad fin-like **Roque de Huso** (see Walk 34). Returning to Wp.6, we zigzag up to a signposted junction (Wp.8 55M) where we turn right to return to the start (60M).

Bejenado is the solitary peak at the southern end of the **Caldera**. Though not unusually high, its singular position makes it one of the best *miradors* in La Palma, no small distinction on an island boasting an embarrassment of outstanding views. The path, which is straightforward and well-waymarked (yellow-and-white stripes), is so gradually staged, one barely notices the climb. Walking shoes or trainers are adequate. Not to be done on hot, windy days when there's a risk of fire.

Short Version: to **El Rodeo** (both linear or circular possible)

Access: by car
Set the odometer at zero at the start of the **LP-302**, into the **Parque Nacional**. Ignore branches to **Virgen del Pino** and **La Cumbrecita** (km0.8 & km1) and follow the main road (**LP-3021** after **La Cumbrecita** turn-off), through the **El Barrial** *urbanización*. At km4.5 the tarmac ends. Ignoring 'Calle Valencia' that forks to the right here and passing a commercial mini-bus unmarked bus-stop right after it, continue on the main dirt track, **Pista de Valencia**, signposted 'PR-13.3 Bejenado'. At km5.8 the tarmac resumes. Park round the next corner (km6) at a mapboard detailing the route.

Our start at Pista Valencia

From the parking area (Wp.1 0M), we take the dirt track (**Pista Valencia**) (not yet **Pista Ferrer** as the signpost and mapboard show) climbing to the left, and within a few minutes come to a **Pista de Ferrer** junction (Wp.2 10M). To the right is our return route. We bear left, soon coming into sight of **Bejenado**.

Ignoring all branches, we follow the main track as it bears west, pass along two volcanic tubes in a rock, until we reach a signposted junction (Wp.3 37M), where we leave the track and climb to the right (N) on a pine-needle covered trail (to the left is a 1.2km detour to the petroglyphs of **Lomo Gordo**).

Petroglyphs seen on the detour

The itinerary is driveable to Wp.3, but the walk starts lower down to avoid congestion on a track that could, literally, be vital in the event of fire. Even

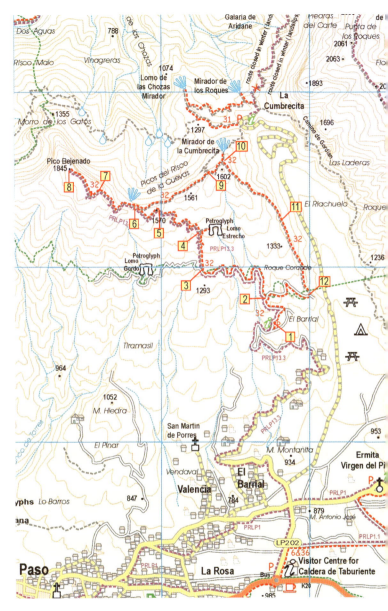

Spaniards, who generally don't get out of their car till it's tipping over a precipice, seem to respect the norm.

The trail climbs along a fence and soon dwindles to a path winding steadily up a broad spur defined by two gullies. At another signposted junction (Wp.4 46M) we bear right for a five minute diversion to visit the 'petroglyphs' of **Lomo Estrecho** … well, one actually and that's behind bars, but it's only 120 metres away so you may as well visit it! Returning to Wp.4, we cross the westernmost gully defining the spur and continue climbing steadily (NW), crossing and, in one case, re-crossing three more gullies, the third of which, below the **Risco de las Cuevas**, is distinguished by a quadruple watershed (Wp.5 65M).

A few metres before the *pico*

Ignoring a faint cairn-marked branch to the right, we climb to the rim of **El Rodeo** (Wp.6 75M), a natural balcony from where we have our first stunning views of the **Caldera**.

Continuing our steady climb on a narrower, rougher path,

Enjoying views from the peak

we zigzag up the back of the peak, bringing Tenerife, La Gomera and El Hierro into view. After climbing through more switchbacks than I'd care to count, we come to a longish, north-easterly stretch, crossing a final gully (Wp.7 100M).

The remaining long zigzags lead us up to the crest, which is mildly vertiginous, and the summit of **Pico Bejenado** (Wp.8 117M), where we have a superb panorama over the **Caldera**, including the sacred pinnacle of **Roque Idafe**.

After enjoying the views, we return to the **El Rodeo** junction (Wp.6) and turn left, heading in an eastern direction along the rim for 'Pista de Valencia por Roque de los Cuervos'. After 1km, we reach a junction to **La Cumbrecita** (Wp.9 160M), where we maintain direction, staying on the ridge. Our trail dips up and down, traversing sparse pine forest before climbing onto a spur where we come to a turn-off for **Roque de los Cuervos** (Wp.10 166M) (just a stone's throw away and worth the detour).

Returning to Wp.10, we start our descent, following signs for 'Pista de Valencia'. The path curls between tall pine trees as great views open out below our feet. After descending through several switchbacks, we pass a cluster of boulders (Wp.11 190M). Twenty minutes later we bear right (NW) at a signposted junction (Wp.12 210M) to join the **Pista de Ferrer** dirt track. After 80 metres, we ignore a broad but indistinct track to the left and carry straight on, following the poorly waymarked **Pista de Ferrer** into a rocky hollow. The track climbs gently above a *barranco* to bring us back to Wp.2 a good 10 minutes later, from where we follow our outward route on **Pista Valencia** back to Wp.1 (230M).

A classic route up the aptly named **Barranco de las Angustias**, literally 'Ravine of Anguishes', more pithily translated as 'Gorge of Fear'; either way, you get the picture. This is the supreme ravine on an island of ravines, worn through the western wall of the **Caldera** before the crater's water was canalised. Canals notwithstanding, freak flash floods are not unknown, so check the forecast at the **Visitors' Centre** first, and don't set off with an optimistic "Oh, it's only a bit cloudy" attitude since the authorities close the ravine even if there's only a slight drizzle.

The *cascada* is a small waterfall stained by deposits from the ferruginous water. The described route follows the official path, which is well signposted, but staying in the bed of the *barranco* is an enjoyable alternative in summer (see text).

NB GPS reception is poor (hence the dearth of waypoints), but once you're on trail, the route is obvious and well signposted.

Access by car:
NB Though surfaced, the road into the *barranco* is steep, narrow and tortuous. It is not recommended for nervous drivers. Come to that, it's not recommended for cavalier drivers, either! From **Los Llanos de Aridane**, we follow the **LP-214** and signs for **Parque Nacional Caldera de Taburiente**. We park alongside the bed of the *barranco* a little over 2.2km after the park information cabin.

Our start at Wp.1

The walk starts 150 metres later on a narrow path along the left bank of the *barranco*, marked with a 'PR-13' signpost and, more usefully since these signs continue inside the park, a green panel for '*zona de acampada*' (Wp.1 0M). The path soon joins a dirt track, which we follow (NE) into the *barranco*.

When the track passes under an aqueduct and climbs north, we stay in the barranco (Wp.2 10M). For the next 90 minutes, we simply follow the *Zona Acampada* signs until we reach the dam at **Dos Aguas**.

Trudging up the gravelly bed of the increasingly narrow ravine, we criss-cross a meagre, weedy rivulet then, 100 metres after a tiny (frequently dry) affluent trickling down a stepped cascade to our right, take a signposted path to the left (Wp.3 25M).

Ignoring a rough track branching left after a few metres, we cross the affluent **Barranco del Fraile** (Wp.4 30M) then, five minutes later, the main watercourse. Climbing onto the left bank, we pass an overgrown path up to a small house on the right (visible from lower down, but not from the junction).

Our path returns to the *barranco* where, fifty metres before an aqueduct, we bear left and climb steadily. Crossing a canal at its junction with the aqueduct (45M), we follow the canal for a while, then cross it again, passing the **Morro de la Era** cabin and crossing a dry torrent streaked with water stains. Re-crossing the *barranco* (60M), we climb very slightly through pine and prickly pear before a stretch of concrete brings us back down to the riverbed (65M). Fifty metres after passing a path to **El Carbón** on our left, we bear right, away from the streambed, and cross the **Lomo de la Rosera** (70M).

The path rejoins the streambed (and it is a stream by now) just before a piped aqueduct fitted with slats to serve as a footbridge. We go under the aqueduct (Wp.5 85M) and follow the stream, the weed already rusty with iron deposits, passing a tiny water hut squeezed under a huge boulder. From here, we can either take the signposted path (to the left) along the watercourse's raised right bank or stay beside the stream for 150 metres until we reach the turbine hut and dam at **Dos Aguas**, where we climb through the trees to the left of the dam. In either case, we emerge in a large open area just behind the dam where the **Río Taburiente** and **Barranco Almendro Amargo** ('bitter almonds') run into one another to form the **Barranco de la Angustias** (Wp.6 100M). Immediately after crossing a stone wall, we ford the **Río Taburiente**, and carry straight on.

Continuing up the **Barranco Almendro Amargo**, we pass a signposted path (Wp.7 110M) onto a bankside shelf, an alternative route to **Playa de Taburiente** (Walk 34).

Ignoring this branch, we stay in the streambed, splashing along and clambering over an outcrop of rock, by-passing a narrow water-chute to reach the **Cascada de Colores** (Wp.8 125M), which is pretty but not exactly a kaleidoscope, the principal colours being shades of orange and green.

Cascada de Colores

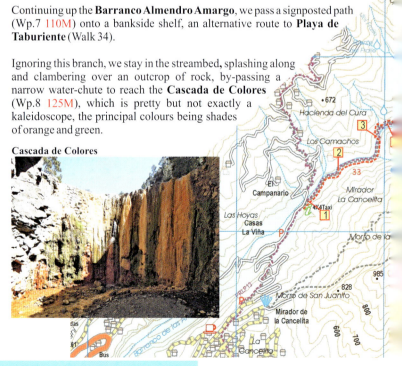

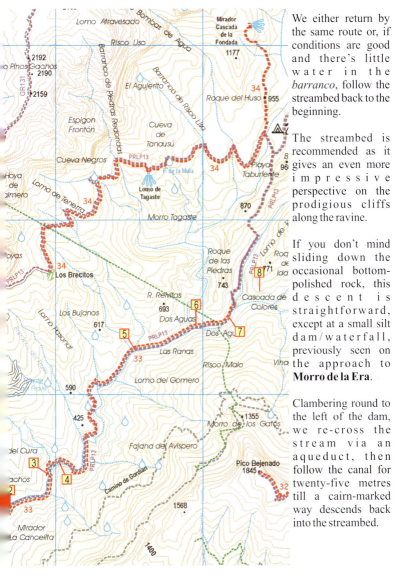

We either return by the same route or, if conditions are good and there's little water in the *barranco*, follow the streambed back to the beginning.

The streambed is recommended as it gives an even more impressive perspective on the prodigious cliffs along the ravine.

If you don't mind sliding down the occasional bottom-polished rock, this descent is straightforward, except at a small silt dam/waterfall, previously seen on the approach to **Morro de la Era**.

Clambering round to the left of the dam, we re-cross the stream via an aqueduct, then follow the canal for twenty-five metres till a cairn-marked way descends back into the streambed.

During the approach to Wp.3, look out for a couple of faint petroglyphs on a rock to the right.

A walking holiday on La Palma wouldn't be complete without a day in the Caldera and in this itinerary we combine the easiest route to the **Casas de Taburiente** campsite with a strenuous climb to the most spectacular viewing point inside the crater, the **Mirador de la Cascada Fondada**.

'**Playa' de Taburiente** is not actually a beach, but a confluence of watercourses where impromptu dams frame shallow plunge-pools. A very slight risk of vertigo en route to the campsite becomes strong on the way up to the *mirador*, though the most vertiginous spots have handrails or railings. Start early during the summer as the caldera really is a cauldron in the afternoon. Don't be deceived by the gentle descent to the playa. It's still 300 metres to be climbed at the end of the day. For an exciting new variation on this classic itinerary, see the extension below.

Short version: to **Playa de Taburiente** 3 walker / 480 metres

Extension: our new version of this itinerary offers an exciting alternative ending (particularly useful if your stay is limited and you want to do as much walking as you can each day) that links up with Walk 33 for the ultimate **Caldera** adventure. However, since you will be arriving at the 'wrong' end of the ravine for abandoning Walk 33 in its early stages in the event of rain, it is absolutely essential to check the forecast first. 5 walker / 915 metres

Access by car:
From **Los Llanos de Aridane** follow the **LP-214** and signs for **Parque Nacional Caldera de Taburiente** then take the **Los Brecitos** track to the small parking area at the end, 10.3 kilometres from the bed of the ravine. If you don't have your own vehicle or intend linking up with Walk 33, inquire at the **Los Llanos de Aridane** tourism office (922 402 528 / 922 402 583) about 4x4 taxis.

From the **Los Brecitos** parking area, we take the 'turnstile' wooden-railed path descending behind the mapboard (Wp.1 0M). Ignoring all branches, we follow this well-signposted path all the way to the *playa* (signposted 'Zona de Acampada'), so if you take no great pleasure from being told what you're doing, close the book now and open it again in 80 minutes.

Los Brecitos parking area and Wp.1

The path descends to the first of seven bridges, the fourth of which crosses **Barranco del Ciempies** (Wp.2 10M). Winding along a contour line, we cross **Barranco de las Cañeras** , after which views open out to the south and we traverse **Lomo de Tenerra,** passing a fork off to the left leading to a house that is visible behind the pine trees (Wp.3 20M).

After a steady descent, we cross **Barranco de las Piedras Redondas** (Wp.4 35M), literally 'round stones', a somewhat inadequate description for the massive lumps of volcanic agglomerate littering the ravine.

Mirador del Lomo de Tagasaste

Continuing our steady descent, we pass the **Mirador del Lomo de Tagasaste** (Wp.5 40M) (from where we can see **Pico Bejenado** Walk 32) and the **Fuente de la Mula o de la Faya** (Wp.6 45M).

Our next bridge (Wp.7 60M) is over the **Barranco de Risco Liso**, immediately after which we pass a path branching left to petroglyphs.

After the bridgeless **Barranco de Bombas de Agua** (Wp.8 70M), the sound of trickling water gradually grows to a roar as we glimpse the **Río Taburiente** way below us and the campsite comes into view. We then descend to a junction just above **Playa de Taburiente** (Wp.9 80M), where the path to the cascade, signposted 'Hoyo Verde', branches left.

For the short version and link to Walk 33
We bear right here, crossing the main river to follow the yellow and white waymarked path for 250 metres to the campsite and **Centro de Servicios de Taburiente** information centre.

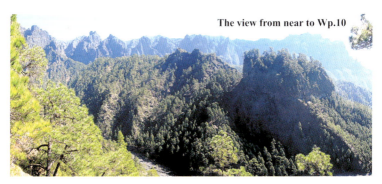

The view from near to Wp.10

For the main walk
We turn left, then fork left at a Y-junction for **Hoyo Verde/Cascada de la Fondada**. After zigzagging steadily then steeply up to **Roque del Huso** (Wp.10 100M), we negotiate our first vertiginous stretch helped by a steel handrail and wooden railings, then climb behind the *roque* onto the ridge (Wp.11 110M) we follow to the north. Once again, you can safely ignore the

text, so long as you also ignore the occasional minor branch paths and bear in mind there are several vertiginous stretches.

Climbing along the ridge, we pass a very narrow stretch with a chain handrail, then skirt a rocky outcrop, where the path is lined with stumpy posts that are more hazard than help.

After another outcrop and more stumpy posts, we climb steadily alongside a watercourse to a Y-junction (Wp.12 130M). The branch to the right is a shortcut that doesn't really shorten or cut anything, so we bear left on the main path, climbing steadily along the right bank of the watercourse.

We then switch back to the left bank below a couple of bewigged boulders for a final brief climb to the **Mirador Cascada de la Fondada** (Wp.13 140M).

The water is meagre, but the fall is immense. We can either return by the same route or extend the itinerary to link up with Walk 33.

Extension
To link up with Walk 33, at Wp.9 we cross the main river to follow the yellow and white waymarked path for 250 metres to the

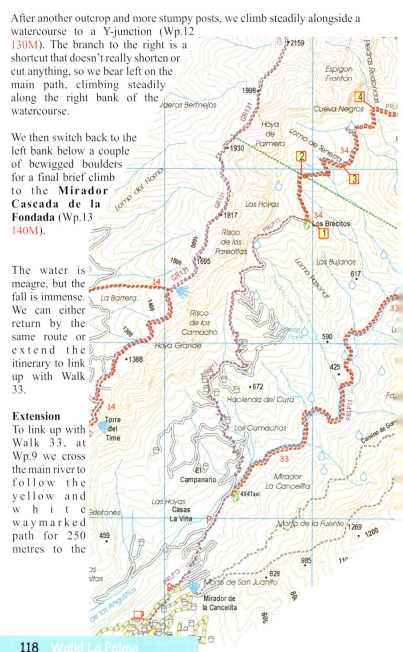

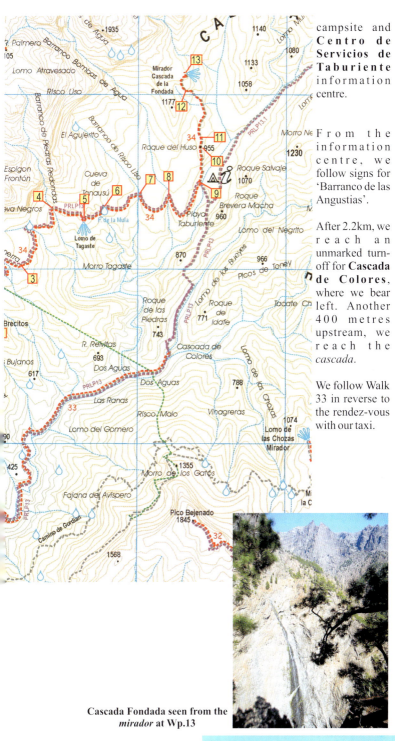

campsite and **Centro de Servicios de Taburiente** information centre.

From the information centre, we follow signs for 'Barranco de las Angustias'.

After 2.2km, we reach an unmarked turn-off for **Cascada de Colores**, where we bear left. Another 400 metres upstream, we reach the *cascada*.

We follow Walk 33 in reverse to the rendez-vous with our taxi.

Cascada Fondada seen from the *mirador* **at Wp.13**

This tour is an ideal introduction to the immediate surroundings of La Palma's capital **Santa Cruz**, its enchanting narrow streets, and some of the remaining sections of the old Royal Way or *camino real,* which connected the east of the island with the **Aridane** valley in the west. En route, we visit an amazing lookout point at the **Mirador de la Concepción** and (on the **Ruta de los Molinos** (Route of the Mills), also known as the **Ruta del Agua** or Water Route, the remarkable watermills that were so vital in the history of harnessing the island's hydraulic potential after the Spanish conquest.

The walk is also a gastronomic extravaganza, as several highly rated restaurants are en route. As with all walks that involve crossing built up areas, the description may seem dauntingly detailed, but it's worth persevering to explore the rich history of the island's capital and its immediate hinterland.

* **Chipi-Chipi** is considered one of best restaurants on the island, but we have also heard positive recommendations for the **Restaurante Casa Osmunda** and **Restaurante El Meson** near the **Mirador de la Concepción**.

Access:
By car, bus, and (for those staying in **Santa Cruz de la Palma**) on foot. The walk starts from **Plaza de España**, the historic centre of **Santa Cruz**. If arriving by car, the most abundant parking options are on the waterfront, 100 metres east of the starting point. If arriving by bus, follow the **Calle O'Daly** pedestrian zone from the main bus station; the starting point is about 400 metres north-east of the bus station.

Plaza de España, our start point

From the charming **Plaza de España** (Wp.1 0M), which architecturally and historically is one of the island's most important squares, we climb the broad stairway between the church and the fountain. In front of the **Biblioteca Municipal**, we turn left and climb a cobbled lane. Crossing the small **Plaza San Sebastian**, we carry straight on up **Calle San Sebastian**.

After a steady climb, we reach a neat *plaza* with an ancient water trough (Wp.2 7M see photo over the page) under a white house with a carved wooden balcony. This *dornajo* (water trough or manger) was a traditional watering hole for pilgrims, traders and muleteers using the *camino real*. It was also used as a *lavadero* or washhouse.

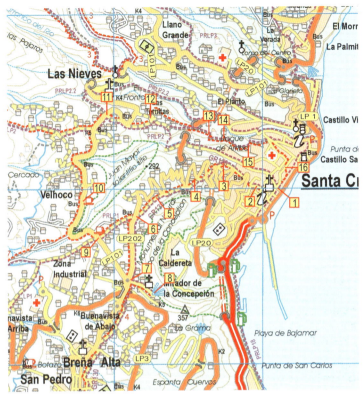

The plaza at Wp.2

We continue climbing on another broad stairway (**Calle Tosquitas**, which starts next to an old house with a pink facade) until we reach a main road, **Carretera Timibúcar** (the **LP-202**), which we will later re-cross several times.

Lane between Wps. 2 and 3

Turning right, we follow the road for 50 metres, then turn sharp left on a narrow, much patched lane (**Calle Montecristo**), which soon joins **Calle Calsinas**. Following the **GR-130** and **PR-LP1** waymarks, we re-cross the road a few minutes later, climbing stairs to a short paved section that almost immediately deposits us back on the road again, this time in front of a blue water-management building (*Aguas Potables*).

Molinos de Bellido (from Wp.3)

Bearing left, then right thirty metres later, we continue to follow **Calle Calsinas**. 150 metres further on, at a sharp left-hand bend in the road, we reach a lookout point (Wp.3 24M), from where we have great views of the water mills we visit later on.

Climbing steadily on a tarmac lane (**Calle la Cuesta**), we pass multi-coloured houses then, just before reaching the road again, bear left between garden fences on another patchily repaired lane that passes an ochre coloured house, **La Casa Vieja**.

Re-crossing the road, we reach a well preserved paved section of the original *camino real*, where there's an information panel and a water tap (Wp.4 35M). We then briefly join the road and follow it for 40 metres, after which we branch off to the left (still on **Calle la Cuesta**).

The steep lane soon passes a pastry shop (**Dulcería Emir**), then a botanical garden with a small zoo **Maroparque** (Wp.5 48M). Immediately after passing a small square with a shrine, we reach the main road (Wp.6 53M).

A section of the original *camino real* (Wp.4)

The main itinerary carries straight on at this junction, but first it's worth detouring to take in another great viewing point, the **Mirador de la Concepción**. Bearing left, we follow the **GR-130** alongside the road to a roundabout (Wp.7 66M), just before the **Restaurante Casa Osmunda**. Turning left, we pass a playground and climb first to a chapel, then to the lookout point of **Mirador de la Concepción** (Wp.8 76M). From here we have a splendid view of **Santa Cruz** and its port. The *mirador* also used to be the site of a lighthouse, to which sailors would climb and make offerings to the Virgin, hoping for protection and good luck.

Returning to the junction at Wp.6, we follow the **PR-LP1 (Camino la Estrella)** (SW) up to the **Restaurante Donde La Graja** (Wp.9 101M).

Turning right, we continue on **Carretera las Nieves** (**LP-101**), passing the **Restaurante Chipi-Chipi** (Wp.10 113M) and a large white shrine. At a signposted turn-off for the **Ruta de los Molinos** (Wp.11 136M), just before the **Restaurante Los Almendros**, we leave the road, bearing right on the **PR-LP2/2.2** (direction 'Santa Cruz' and 'Barranco de la Virgen') which descends a steep concrete lane marked as a dead-end.

We soon rejoin the road in front of a satellite pylon, but leave it a few metres to the right, where we take a narrow concrete lane that leads to a Y junction (Wp.12 147M). The right hand branch is a shorter alternative way back to **Santa Cruz**, but we fork left on the **PR-LP2.2 Ruta de los Molinos** to see the mills. After 150 metres, we turn sharp right on a wider lane tucked between a fence and a wall.

Five minutes later, when the lane bends sharply to the left and we see a football field directly below us in a ravine, we bear right on a footpath marked by an information board. Passing under a thick water pipe, we carry on, following thinner pipes and a disused concrete channel. The trail passes another information board (Wp.13 161M) at the **Bellido Mills**, where the settlers first exploited hydraulic power for milling grain. We then pass a turn-off for **Santa Cruz** (Wp.14 172M) and continue straight on, following a narrow path protected by a railing at its most exposed stretch above the *barranco*, before returning to the streets of **Santa Cruz** (Wp.15 180M).

Turning left, we follow **Calle Olen**, at the end of which we bear right then, after 80 metres, descend a stairway slightly to the left. Joining **Calle El Pilar**, we descend past a school to reach the **Copacabana Bar**, in front of which we turn right then immediately left on stairs descending to a pedestrianised cobbled lane (Wp.16 192M). From here we continue letting gravity do its work and, less than 100 metres later, bear left onto **Calle Doctor Santos Abreu** then left again after 35 metres onto **Calle Vandale**. At the next corner, we turn right to join **Calle Anselmo Peréz de Brito**, which brings us back to **Plaza de España**.

Our start (Wp.1)

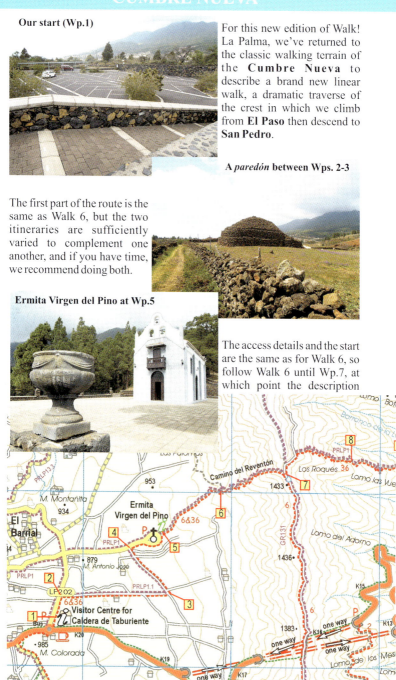

For this new edition of Walk! La Palma, we've returned to the classic walking terrain of the **Cumbre Nueva** to describe a brand new linear walk, a dramatic traverse of the crest in which we climb from **El Paso** then descend to **San Pedro**.

A *paredón* between Wps. 2-3

The first part of the route is the same as Walk 6, but the two itineraries are sufficiently varied to complement one another, and if you have time, we recommend doing both.

Ermita Virgen del Pino at Wp.5

The access details and the start are the same as for Walk 6, so follow Walk 6 until Wp.7, at which point the description below kicks in. The first seven waypoints of Walk 6 have been incorporated into the waypoint file for this itinerary.

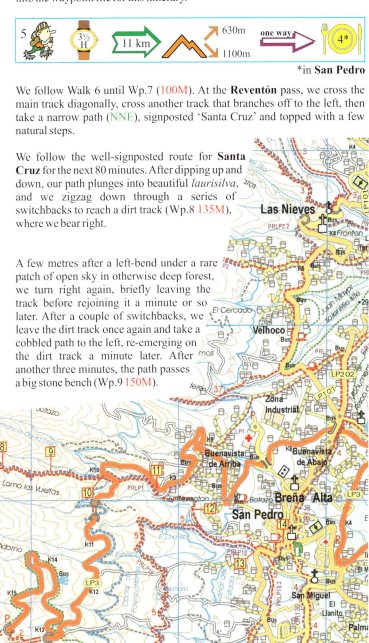

5 | 3½ H | 11 km | 630m / 1100m | one way | 4*

*in **San Pedro**

We follow Walk 6 until Wp.7 (100M). At the **Reventón** pass, we cross the main track diagonally, cross another track that branches off to the left, then take a narrow path (NNE), signposted 'Santa Cruz' and topped with a few natural steps.

We follow the well-signposted route for **Santa Cruz** for the next 80 minutes. After dipping up and down, our path plunges into beautiful *laurisilva*, and we zigzag down through a series of switchbacks to reach a dirt track (Wp.8 135M), where we bear right.

A few metres after a left-bend under a rare patch of open sky in otherwise deep forest, we turn right again, briefly leaving the track before rejoining it a minute or so later. After a couple of switchbacks, we leave the dirt track once again and take a cobbled path to the left, re-emerging on the dirt track a minute later. After another three minutes, the path passes a big stone bench (Wp.9 150M).

Laurisilva (Wps. 7-8)

15 minutes later, we pass another bench in the same half-arch style, then cross a canal and join the main road (the LP-3) (Wp.10 170M).

Turning left, we follow the road for 60 metres, then cross onto a footpath on the right, which soon zigzags down to emerge under an impressive cave high up a rock face. A hundred metres after the cave, we leave the **Santa Cruz** path (the **PR-LP 1**) and turn right for **San Pedro** (signposted 'Fuentes de la Breña') (Wp.11 182M).

Following a stone-paved path flanked by low walls, we descend a dry *barranco,* passing an aqueduct five minutes later. After another five minutes, the footpath runs into a concrete lane (Wp.12 194M) beside a house. Continuing in a south-easterly direction, we pass under another aqueduct and join the **PR-LP19 Camino de las Fuentes**.

Continuing down the lane, following the trail to **San Pedro**, we ignore all branches until we reach the main road (**LP-202**) above a tunnel (Wp.13 209M). Turning left on the main road, we stroll along the pavement to reach the main square in **San Pedro** (Wp.14 214M).

San Pedro main square

Being the steepest walk in a book about the steepest island in the world, this challenging excursion won't be to everybody's taste. You need plenty of stamina, have to be ready for a bit of scrambling, and will probably find that you are pushing yourself to your absolute limits. Naturally, the extreme nature of the walk is also a large part of the reward. Add to that beautiful pine and laurel forests, stunning views into the national park, and an immense sense of having achieved something significant, and you have an itinerary that, for the right sort of temperament, is an exhilarating adventure. A glance at the summary data will tell you if this is the walk for you. The route is very slippery after rain and hiking poles are recommended in all conditions.

Alternative: If you want to avoid the steepest part of the walk, which is the return route, continue south from Wp.7 (the signposted junction of the **PR-LP2.1** and **GR-131**), following the **GR-131** for another 2.6km until the **Reventón** pass. From there, take the **PR-LP1** (see Walk 36) in an eastern direction down to **Velhoco** or **San Pedro** (**Breña Alta**).

Access:
By car or by bus N°303 (circular line starting from the main bus station in **Santa Cruz**). The walk starts in **Velhoco** from the large shrine (the only one on this stretch of road) at the km5 marker on the **LP-101**, seventy metres south-west of the bus-stop. Motorists should park just below the bus stop on the hard shoulder. Other parking options are along the main road between **Chipi-Chipi** restaurant (one of the best restaurants on the island) and the shrine.

The shrine at our start point

From the shrine at km5 of the **LP-101** (Wp.1 0M), we take a concrete lane heading west, away from the main road, following the yellow-and-white signs for 'La Tabladita' via the **PR-LP2**. The lane, which is lined with *nispero*, avocado and chestnut trees, winds past scattered houses and their driveways.

Ignoring an asphalted branch climbing to the right, we bear left at a Y junction (Wp.2 4M), and continue our gentle ascent, passing some minor tracks forking off to the left a little while later. After passing a huge solitary pine tree, we leave behind the last terraced fields and orange groves, as well as the concrete, and turn right on the **Camino Lomo del Lance** trail (Wp.3 23M).

The trail shadows neat dry-stone walls, then begins climbing steadily,

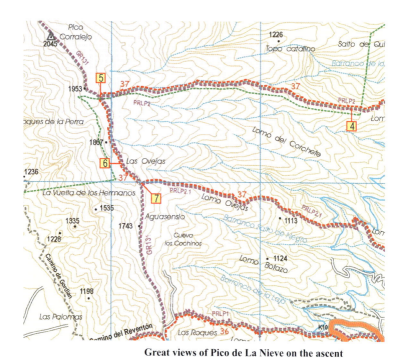

Great views of Pico de La Nieve on the ascent

narrowing to a pine-needle carpeted path and gaining elevation through a series of tight switchbacks.

The path only levels out briefly, the second time in front of a tall rock formation (Wp.4 72M) that we pass to the left. Climbing along a distinct ridge, we get great

On the final ascent

views to the right through the scattered pine toward the barren top of **Pico de la Nieve**.

During the lengthy ascent the footpath rarely levels out, steepening each time ever more mercilessly, but there are no junctions and nowhere to go wrong as we just keep on climbing until we finally reach the main ridge and the **GR-131** (Wp.5 171M) where we enjoy a well deserved break.

Turning left (S) (signposted 'Refugio del

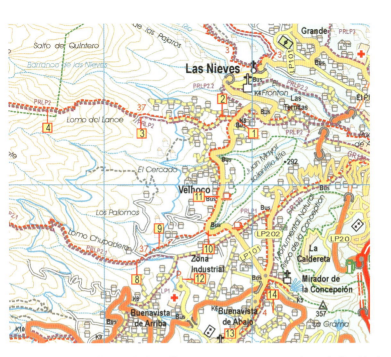

Pilar'), we follow the long distance **GR-131**, an easy path neatly lined by lava stones, descending gently along the edge of the national park, which drops away to our right.

Our efforts to get up here are amply rewarded by sweeping views of the island's only stand-alone summit, **Pico Bejenado** to our right, and (in the distance ahead of us) the first leg of the popular **Ruta de los Volcanes**.

On the right day we can also see a stunning spectacle staged by nature as the moisture-carrying trade winds push bands of cloud over the **Cumbre Nueva** ridge, where they break and flow down to create the unique flora that is such a feature of this part of the island.

a stunning spectacle ..

Enjoying the views, we soon reach a signposted turn-off (Wp.6 186M) to an indistinct summit, **Pico de las Ovejas**, which is just a few metres to the right. Continuing down the ridge, we reach a junction with the **PR-LP2.1** (Wp.7 190M) where we turn left for 'Bco. de Juan Mayor' and begin our steep descent (E). Take care here. The descent is very steep and, especially after rain, very slippery. If it is wet, best opt for the alternative mentioned in the introduction, continuing on the GR until the **Reventón** pass to take the **PR-LP1** toward **Santa Cruz**. The first leg from **Reventón** overlaps with Walk 36 and later joins the **PR-LP2.1** just before **Velhoco**.

Otherwise, we turn left at Wp.7, initially descending between shrubs and pines, then through 'tunnels' of thicket where the trail is sometimes overgrown with ferns, soon entering the shade of dense laurel forest. This stretch of the itinerary is little used and occasionally overhanging branches may slow down our progress. At one point, we wind through an almost pitch-black forest before reaching a natural lookout window, where we get the first fine views of the coast since starting our descent. The footpath then plunges back into shadowy forest, in which we cross a covered canal.

A few minutes after the canal, a stony stairway brings us onto a dirt track that ends in an adjacent meadow where there is a waterworks construction. GPS reception is poor here, hence no waypoint.

Turning sharp left, we follow the dirt track for 200 metres to a Y junction under the breathtaking vertical rockface of **Barranco de Juan Mayor**. Turning sharp right (SE), we continue descending on a broader track, with the rockface on our left, where some incredibly tenacious trees are growing out of what appears to be the almost vertical wall of the *barranco*. As the ravine widens, we walk along a dry stream-bed, soon leaving behind the first (abandoned) buildings seen on our descent.

Passing a large reservoir, we bear right at a Y-junction (Wp.8 284M) on a slightly better dirt track. After passing the high walls of terraced fields on our right and going under an aqueduct leading to a house, we reach a crossroads with a concrete lane (Wp.9 290M), where we continue straight on, descending a tarmac lane lined with lampposts. After 180 metres, we ignore a branch to the left and continue along the lane until it joins the main road (Wp.10 300M) where we bear left.

We now simply follow the main road back to Wp.1. If you arrived by bus, you can skip this rather uninspiring stretch of road walking and catch the return bus from one of the stops along the main road. However, if you have the time and energy, it's worth continuing on the road a little further to enjoy one of the island's very best restaurants, **Chipi-Chipi** (Wp.11 305M). Thereafter, another good kilometre on the road brings us back to the shrine and the start of the walk (Wp.1).

BUS INFORMATION
www.transporteslapalma.com

TAXIS
+34 686 55 38 68 www.taxilapalma.com

ACCIDENT AND EMERGENCY
Tel. 112

CASH
There is currently no cashpoint at the airport, so don't rely on withdrawing money there on arrival.

THINGS TO DO

STARGAZING
Astrotour
Tel +34 922 430625 www.astrotour.es

AstroCamp
Tel +34 922 410431 www.astrolapalma.com

PARAGLIDING
Palmaclub, Puerto Naos
 Tel +34 610 695750 www.palmaclub.com

NATOUR
provides bus transport for self-guided walks (guided walks also available).
Tel +34 922 433001 www.natour-trekking.com

VULKANO TOURS
offers tours of volcanic tubes
Tel +34 609 767496 www.vulkanotours.com

BIKE RENTAL
Bike Station La Palma, Av. de la Cruz Roja, 3, Puerto de Naos
Tel +34 922 408355

EL ROQUE DE LOS MUCHACHOS OBSERVATORY
The telescopes at El Roque de los Muchachos are not usually open to the public but there are occasional tours. Contact the Astrophysics Institute of the Canaries for details and book well in advance of your trip
Tel +34922 425 700 www.iac.es

WEBSITES

GENERAL INFORMATION
www.visitlapalma.es
www.turismodecanarias.com

WALKING INFORMATION
www.senderosdelapalma.com

La Palma Tour & Trail Super-Durable Map by David Brawn (pub. Discovery Walking Guides Ltd) £8.99 For the latest edition see: www.dwgwalking.co.uk/lap.htm

A Breathtaking Window on the Universe by Sheila Crosby An introduction to the observatory and stargazing on La Palma £15.00 www.dragontree.sheilacrosby.com

A Field Guide to the Birds of the Atlantic Islands: Canary Islands, Madeira, Azores, Cape Verde by Tony Clarke, Chris Orgill, Tony Disley (£26.99 Pub: Christopher Helm Publishers Ltd 30 Jun. 2006) ISBN: 9780713660234

Field Guide to the Birds of Macaronesia: Azores, Madeira, Canary Islands, Cape Verde by Eduardo Garcia-Del-Rey (£20.94 Pub: Lynx Edicions 1 May 2011) ISBN: 9788496553712

Native Flora of the Canary Islands by Miguel Angel Cabrera Perez (Author), Martin Gell (Translator) (£8.13 Pub: Editorial Everest 31 Dec. 2000) ISBN: 9788424135553

TOURIST INFORMATION OFFICES / CENTROS DE INFORMACIÓN

Tazacorte
Casa del Artesano
Isidro Guadalupe 2 - El Charco
(near the Church of San Miguel)
Tazacorte 38700
Tel.:+34 922480151/922480803
turismo@tazacorte.es
www.tazacorte.es

Santa Cruz de La Palma
Avda. Blas Pérez González, s/n
opposite the post office)
Santa Cruz de la Palma 38700
Tel: +34 922412106
oitsantacruz@lapalmacit.com

Los Llanos de Aridane
Avda. Doctor Flemming, s/n
Los Llanos de Aridane 38760
Tel: +34 922402583
oitaridane@lapalma.cit.com
www.lapalmacit.com

El Paso
Antonio Pino Pérez, s/n
El Paso 38750
Tel: +34 922485733
oitelpaso@lapalmacit.com
www.lapalmacit.com

Los Cancajos
Punta de la Arena, 4
Breña Baja 38712
Tel: +34 922181354
oitloscancajos@lapalmacit.com
www.lapalmacit.com

Puerto Naos
(Office is in the Car park at
the entrance to Puerto Naos)
Los Llanos de Aridane 38760
Tel: +34 618856516
oitpuertonaos@lapalmacit.com
www.lapalmacit.com

Fuencaliente
Pza.Minerva, s/n
Fuencaliente 38740
Tel: +34 922444003
oitfuencaliente@hotmail.com

B BUS INFORMATION

Bus timetables are subject to frequent changes, so please regard the following as a guide only. We suggest you ask on arrival for the latest information, from **Tourist Information Offices** or from the Bus Station, Avenida Los Indianos, 3, 38700 Santa Cruz de la Palma. Phone: +34 922 41 19 24 www.transporteslapalma.com

100
CIRCULAR S/C DE LA PALMA - BARLOVENTO - STO DOMINGO - TAZACORTE - LOS LLANOS
hourly from 15 past the hour weekdays to 22.30
2-hourly weekends/fiestas from 06.15 to 21.15

100
CIRCULAR LOS LLANOS - TAZACORTE - STO DOMINGO - BARLOVENTO - S/C DE LA PALMA
hourly from 15 minutes past the hour weekdays to 21.15
2-hourly weekends/fiestas from 07.15 to 20.15

101
S/C DE LA PALMA - MIRCA CIRCULAR
leaving from LA DENESA: 07.15
leaving from MIRCA hourly from 45 minutes past the hour weekdays to 21.45
leaving from MIRCA 2-hourly weekends/fiestas from 08.45 to 20.45

200
S/C DE LA PALMA - SAN JOSÉ - LEDAS - MAZO - FUENCALIENTE - LOS LLANOS CIRCULAR
2-hourly weekdays/weekends/fiestas from 08.15 to 22.15

200
LOS LLANOS - FUENCALIENTE - MAZO - LEDAS - SAN JOSÉ - S/C DE LA PALMA CIRCULAR
2-hourly weekdays/weekends/fiestas from 08.15 to 20.15

201
S/C DE LA PALMA - HOYO MAZO - FUENCALIENTE & RETURN
2-hourly weekdays from 07.15 to 21.15
4-hourly weekends/fiestas from 09.15 to 21.15

202
S/C DE LA PALMA - SAN JOSÉ - SAN PEDRO - SAN ISIDRO - LEDS & RETURN
2-hourly weekdays from 09.15 to 21.15
4-hourly weekends/fiestas from 09.15 to 21.15

203
LOS CANARIOS - INDIAS - HOTEL - FARO
from FARO: 2-hourly weekdays/weekends/fiestas from 09.00 to 19.00
from LOS CANARIOS: 2-hourly weekdays/weekends/fiestas from 09.45 to 17.45

204
LOS LLANOS - PTO NAOS - CHARCO VERDE - EL REMO
hourly weekdays/weekends/fiestasfrom 07.30 to 21.30

205
LOS LLANOS - ROSAS - PALOMARES - MANCHAS
2-hourly weekdays only from 07.00 to 13.00, and 14.15

207
LOS LLANOS - PUERTO DE TAZACORTE

hourly weekdays/weekends/fiestas from 07.45 to 21.45

300

S/C DE LA PALMA - LOS LLANOS - HOSPITAL - CUMBRE - EL PASO

half-hourly weekdays from 06.00 to 22.30

hourly weekends/fiestas from 06.30 to 22.30

300

LOS LLANOS - EL PASO - CUMBRE - HOSPITAL - BREÑAS - S/C DE LA PALMA

half-hourly weekdays from 05.30 to 22.30

hourly weekends/fiestas from 06.00 to 22.30

302

S/C DE LA PALMA - VALLE DE LA LUNA - CALSINAS - HOSPITAL - S PEDRO & RETURN

two-hourly weekdays from 07.15 to 21.15

four-hourly weekends/fiestas from 07.15 to 21.15

303

S/C DE LA PALMA - LAS NIEVES - HOSPITAL - S PEDRO - LA GRAMA - CUARTELES - S/C DE LA PALMA (BENAHOARE)

hourly weekdays from 07.15 to 20.15

two-hourly weekends/fiestas from 07.15 to 20.15

303

S/C DE LA PALMA - LA GRAMA - S PEDRO - HOSPITAL - LAS NIEVES - S/C DE LA PALMA (BENAHOARE)

hourly weekdays from 06.45 to 21.45

approximately 2-hourly weekends/fiestas from 07.45 to 20.45

500

S/C DE LAPALMA - CANCAJOS - AIRPORT

half-hourly weekdays from 06.30 to 22.00

approximately hourly weekends /fiestas from 07.00 to 22.00

GLOSSARY

abandonado	abandoned, in poor repair		range
		correos	post office
abierto	open	*cortijo*	farmstead
acampamiento	camping	*costa*	coast
acantilado	cliff	*coto privado de caza*	private hunting area
acequia	water channel		
		Cruz Roja	Red Cross (medical aid)
agua	water		
agua no potable	water (not drinkable)	*cuesta*	slope
		cueva	cave
agua potable	drinking water	*cumbre*	summit
		degollada	pass
alto	high	*derecha*	right (direction)
aparcamiento	parking		
área recreativa	designated picnic spot; may have tables, water	*desprendimiento*	landslide
		embalse	reservoir
		ermita	chapel
		Espacio Natural Protegido	protected area of natural beauty
arroyo	stream		
autopista	main road, motorway		
ayuntamiento	town hall		
bajo	low	*estación de autobus/ guagua*	bus station
barranco	ravine		
bocadillo	bread roll	*farmacia*	chemist
bodegón	inn	*faro*	lighthouse
bosque	wood	*fiesta*	holiday, celebration
cabezo	peak, summit		
cabra montés	mountain goat	*finca*	farm, country house
calle	street	*fuente*	spring
camino	trail, path, track	*gasolinera*	petrol station
		guagua	bus
camino particular	private road	*Guardia Civil*	police
camino real	old donkey trail (lit. royal road)	*guía*	guide
		hostal	hostel, accomm.
carretera	main road	*hoya*	depression (geological)
casa	house		
casa rural	country house accomm.	*iglesia*	church
		información	information
		isla	island
cascada	waterfall	*izquierda*	left (direction)
caserío	hamlet, village	*lago*	lake
		lavadero	laundry area (usually communal)
cementerio	cemetery		
cerrado	closed		
cerro	hill, mountain without a real peak	*librería*	bookshop
		llano	plain
		lluvioso	rainy
cerveza	beer	*lomo*	broad-backed ridge
choza	shelter		
clínica	clinic, hospital	*malpaís*	'bad lands' wild, barren countryside
colmena	bee hive		
comida	food	*mapa*	map
cordillera	mountain	*mercado*	market

mirador	lookout, viewing point	sendero	foot path
montaña	mountain	sierra	mountain range
nublado	cloudy	sin salida	no through road/route
oficina de turismo	tourist office		
parapente	hang-glider	tajo	cliff, escarpment
peligroso	dangerous		
pensión	guesthouse	tapas	bar snacks
pico	peak	tienda	shop
pista	dirt road/track	tinao	typical balcony
pista forestal	forest road/track	típico	traditional
playa	beach		bar/eating place
plaza	square		
policía	police	tormentoso	stormy
pozo	well	torre	tower
prohibido el paso	no entry	torrente	stream
puente	bridge	tubería	water pipe
puerto	port, mountain pass	vallc	valley
		vega	meadow
		ventoso	windy
refugio	refuge, shelter	vereda	path, lane
		vivero	plant nursery, arboretum
río	river, stream		
roque	rock	volcán	volcano
ruta	route	zona recreativa	recreation area
salida	exit		
senda	path, track		

The following index includes place names in Spanish and some of the most commonly used English equivalents.